THE LITTLE BOOK

of

ZEN MONEY

Little Book Series

In the *Little Book* series, the brightest icons in the financial world write on topics that range from tried-and-true investment strategies to tomorrow's new trends. Each book offers a unique perspective on investing, allowing the reader to pick and choose from the very best in investment advice today.

Books in the *Little Book* series include:

The Little Book of Investing Like the Pros by Pearl and Rosenbaum
The Little Book That Still Beats the Market by Joel Greenblatt
The Little Book That Saves Your Assets by David M. Darst
The Little Book That Builds Wealth by Pat Dorsey
The Little Book That Makes You Rich by Louis Navellier
The Little Book of Common Sense Investing by John C. Bogle
The Little Book of Value Investing by Christopher Browne
The Little Book of Big Dividends by Charles B. Carlson
The Little Book of Main Street Money by Jonathan Clements
The Little Book of Trading by Michael W. Covel
The Little Book of Valuation by Aswath Damodaran
The Little Book of Economics by Greg Ip
The Little Book of Sideways Markets by Vitaliy N. Katsenelson
The Little Book of Big Profits from Small Stocks by Hilary Kramer
The Little Book of Currency Trading by Kathy Lien
The Little Book of Bull's Eye Investing by John Mauldin
The Little Book of Emerging Markets by Mark Mobius
The Little Book of Behavioral Investing by James Montier
The Little Book of Hedge Funds by Anthony Scaramucci
The Little Book of Bull Moves by Peter D. Schiff
The Little Book of Alternative Investments by Stein and DeMuth
The Little Book of Bulletproof Investing by Ben Stein and Phil DeMuth
The Little Book of Commodity Investing by John R. Stephenson
The Little Book of the Shrinking Dollar by Addison Wiggin
The Little Book of Stock Market Profits by Mitch Zacks
The Little Book of Safe Money by Jason Zweig

THE LITTLE BOOK

of

ZEN MONEY

A Simple Path to Financial Peace of Mind

By

THE SEVEN DOLLAR MILLIONAIRE

WILEY

Library of Congress Cataloging-in-Publication Data is Available:

ISBN 9781119859673 (Hardback)
ISBN 9781119859680 (ePDF)
ISBN 9781119859697 (ePub)

Cover Design and Image: Wiley

SKYC657EA5A-9126-44FB-8989-DBC98DBF48DC_032822

"Zen is seeing reality directly. . . . It is simply a quiet awareness, without comment, of whatever happens to be here and now."

—Alan Watts, *The Way of Zen*

"The chief task in life is simply this: to identify and separate matters so that I can say clearly to myself which are externals not under my control, and which have to do with the choices I actually control."

—Epictetus, *Discourses*

"It's not about the money, money, money."

—Jessie J, *Price Tag*

Table of Contents

Foreword

I'm so grateful you wrote this book. It's going to be helpful to many people.

Quite a stroke of genius, to combine money with zen. The thing that gets lost in most talks about money is exactly the (for want of a better word) spiritual side of being human. It's high time too that a zen guide, instead of discussing the petals on a dandelion or the segments of an orange, devoted itself to money, a grubby power tool we all use, often without training.

When I was a child, I heard grown-ups tell me that "money isn't important". With hindsight, I think I can see the specific point they were making, which a different spiritual tradition might express thus: "Don't turn money into your God". But I misunderstood. I thought they meant that money was somehow despicable; and for too long I despised it. Today I try to respect it, to see it clearly for what it is. I like to have it coming in, and I like to let it out again.

Your book is big-hearted and righteous, qualities that perhaps derive from the anger that motivated it; but it is also gentle, encouraging, charming, and supremely practical. I wish that I had been able to read it when I was young, and by doing so avoided the agony of fear and shame that hit me in my own personal financial crisis. I hope that many others, finding your book, will avoid that.

John-Paul Flintoff

Acknowledgements

~

Thank you for looking at this little book. Even just considering how you can improve the nature of your financial journey is a brave step, particularly if you have tried before or feel you are starting late. I hope this can help you on your way.

I mention the idyllic Lao town of Luang Prabang a few times in the book, for its serene monastic traditions, but also because it was an important step on my path to writing this book. To thank the town properly, and photographer Kenro Izu who courageously founded the Lao Friends Hospital for Children there, while being more zen than anyone else I know, I will donate any proceeds I receive from book sales to the hospital. If you would like to see or support their amazing work, go to www.fwab.org.

Soo Peng Koh is the most patient designer and illustrator. Who else, when asked for an ensō design, would deliver thousands, taking hours to create them, one fluid sweeping stroke at a time? Thank you so much. Thanks also to the production team at Wiley, Syd and Purvi, for their belief in this project, and their indulgence of my ideas.

I very much want to thank John-Paul Flintoff, author of *How to Change the World,* for his sage advice, which he characteristically won't think was as important as it was, and Tom Hodgkinson, publisher of *The Idler* magazine and author of *How to Be Idle,* for the opportunity to try out a wider range of more relaxed approaches to money in his magazine.

I also need to thank Patrick Jenkins, chair of the Financial Times Financial Literacy and Inclusion Campaign, not just for being so kind as to provide a comment for the book, but also for creating that campaign. It will change lives, Patrick.

There have been far too many other people in my financial education journey to mention: we learn all the time. The migrant workers who attend classes at the Humanitarian Organisation for Migrant Economics (HOME) and ASKI Global in Singapore were an inspiration. At the other end of the spectrum, my very good friend, head of HSBC Equity Strategy and author of *Asian Markets from the Ground Up,* Herald van der Linde, has always been a receptive sounding board for ideas. Meanwhile the investment team at my fund management company make it a regular pleasure to learn new things – something that lies at the heart of a healthy financial journey.

But most of all I need to thank my family, my wife Salina and two daughters, Aliya and Maya, for not laughing at the idea that I could write a book about being zen.

Preface

———————— ∾ ————————

Few subjects feel as far apart as zen and money. This is unfortunate, as bringing a zen approach to our finances can provide answers for many of our money worries. That's what I hope this book can provide.

At one extreme, if we never needed money again, we would have infinite financial peace of mind: we could be blissfully zen about money. At the other, spending every penny, cent or peseta that passes through our lives ensures we will never know that peace.

While never needing money may be as impossible as any zen riddle, or *koan*, the path in that direction offers greater peace than the more travelled one of non-stop spending. I hope this book can help you find your path.

Money

There are simple routes to financial awareness, knowing what money is and the things it can do for us, that can help us all live better lives, and yet so few of us are ever shown these pathways.

We all handle money, often devoting more of our lives than necessary to earning it and then spending it, and yet so little time learning about it. We could be so much more aware of how to use it effectively, how we could make it work for us, and not the other way around.

This simple change in understanding could have a huge impact on the world: on happiness, on mental health, on inequality, and even on the planet itself.

I hope this book can become a gateway to understanding for you, to a simple path without the stress that we so often attach to money.

Zen

As I understand it, the ideas of Buddhism moved from India across China where it became known as "chan" and may have been infused with Taoist ideas before landing in Japan 800 years ago and getting a name-change to "zen". It is argued that the word "dhyana", meaning deep meditation in the Indian tradition, is roughly the same root.

When I think of zen, perhaps like you, I think of that Japanese word as it has taken on a meaning of its own in the West: an exquisite expression of minimalist beauty.

We see it in a perfectly raked rock garden, a broken kintsugi pot mended by strands of gold, or any other wabi-sabi arrangement, the "beautiful sadness" that Nobuo Suzuki describes so perfectly in the subtitle of his book *Wabi Sabi: The Wisdom of Imperfection*.

It is there in the ensō, the ink brushstroke circles that artist and designer Soo Peng Koh so graciously provided for this book. The idea is so simple, to paint a perfect circle, and yet impossible, every single one is different. They are the result of strenuous practice, but a quiet mind. Looking like they show a zero and yet representing infinity, a circle starting back on itself. Almost.

I also gather into this word "zen" one other concept from a quote attributed to Buddha when asked for his most important teaching: "Nothing whatsoever should be clung to."

This is such a powerful phrase that while perhaps not exactly zen in tradition, the emphasis on "nothing" makes it appear very "zen-like" to me, if zen also means minimalist. What could be more minimalist than nothing, after all?

A Little Light

Alan Watts described zen beautifully, and minimally, as "seeing reality directly".

If we see reality directly, at a global and personal level, we must admit that we have real problems with money.

While the number of people in the world living in poverty has dropped significantly over the past few decades, many developed countries still have levels of poverty that are surprisingly high, considering their wealth elsewhere. In some it is even increasing.

The US Census Bureau estimated in 2019 that 10.5% of the population there was living below the poverty line, while the UK government, using a different definition, classified a staggering 23% of households as low income in 2020, up from 18% just a few years before.

People below this line have money stress caused by real money problems, which will mainly be answered by more money. This book, sadly, cannot provide that. If only.

I hope it may provide other answers that will help those people in their journeys: ways to deal with the stress their situation is causing, and some guidance for avoiding these problems in future once they hopefully do have enough money.

For the rest of us, above those lines, our financial stress can perhaps be termed "money worries" or "anxiety" more than "money problems". These worries manifest in many ways, from all kinds of different roots, and range from just uncertainty that delays a positive action, to bad debts built on subsequently regretted decisions, to longer-term disquiet and even shame, among many others.

An almost global lack of formal financial education isn't helping this.

While this financial stress is not as financially restrictive as poverty, it doesn't feel any less real to people suffering it, but rather than insufficient funds being the cause, the biggest problem is that we have never been taught about money. It's like we're in the dark.

As we all know, when the lights are turned on, there's nothing inherently scary about the dark. We can be in a familiar place, but because we can't see everything else as well, we are uncertain. Perhaps even a little frightened. When we try to think about money, we often feel that same fear.

We need to start shining a little light on to money, what it can do for us and what we can do about it. A little light can go a long way.

On a Cliff Edge

Unlike the dark, there's a good reason for our money stress. The persistence and even increase of poverty in the developed world stems in large part from decades of steadily increasing inequality: the Economic Policy Institute calculated that the income of an average CEO increased more than 1,000% between 1978 and 2018, while that of an average worker increased by just 11%. If we assume around 2% inflation, the average CEO's standard of living will have improved by 5 times, the average person's will have halved.

In most English-speaking countries, annual income of the better-off has grown faster than people below them on their income curve. The rich really do keep getting richer.

Income curves and resulting wealth curves have become perilously steep as a result, with fewer people earning good salaries, and a very few owning huge riches: literally stratospheric wealth as they fly into space leaving the rest of us behind.

A curve in a graph is an abstract thing, and when we call it that it might not sound like such a big deal, but it is. This curve is where we all live our lives, earn our incomes and save for a rainy day.

If we visualise the curves we see in the physical world, we might see a nice straight, flat road ahead. It will be easy to get where we want to go.

What cyclists call a "false flat" might be harder: it looks easy when you're in a car but takes a bit more effort to get up when you're on a bike. It could be a gently rolling hill, where you can see there's some effort to get ahead, but you can make that effort.

To bring this back to our income curves, a drop in salary or status in that environment might result in a little fall, but we won't face too big a climb back up again if we need to. These income curves don't necessarily protect weaker or less fortunate members of their societies, but they don't punish them for the smallest mistakes either.

Income curves have tilted up much further, however. In the US, United Kingdom, Australia, and many other countries around the world, most economic growth of the past 40 years has been captured by the wealthy, not the poor. This means the curve has kept on getting steeper.

These forces feel nearly geological in power, and the road ahead is no longer just a sloping curve, it's going almost vertically up a mountain. It might sound like fun if you are at the top, holidaying in a ski villa with a panoramic view beneath you, but living on that curve, day-in and day-out, can feel like standing on a cliff edge.

A lost job, a little crazy spending, or some savings stolen in a scam, and we might run out of money, needing to borrow to make ends meet.

That debt grows quickly, compounding even faster if we have had to resort to non-traditional lenders, and might soon become double or even quadruple the amount we borrowed. It will be hard coming back from that. It could take years. It could take your whole life.

The stress of living on the cliff can make us dizzy, leading to bad decisions, be it gambling on too big a risk, or even just avoidance or denial of the problem, hoping it will go away. Too many people fall foul of "zero-risk fallacy", a cognitive bias that tells us it is possible to have no risks, and that doing nothing may be better than doing something. Doing nothing just leaves us out on the cliff edge. We need to move.

Deep down, everyone on a steep curve feels this stress, from the top of society to the bottom. At the top, there is a pressure to look like your peers, which means spending like the people around you, even if you can't afford it, which can step you out closer to the edge. High performance jobs can lead to stress and over-spending: we see insane competition to get children into the best schools and colleges, leading to scandals, because parents are so worried about their own children on this same curve.

The curve can be at its steepest in the middle, brief glimpses of the "high life" above, giving us nothing but expensive tastes that we can afford by borrowing, while the big drop is still right there at our feet.

Nearer the bottom, the distance seems so enormous to the top that it is out of view, denying any point in trying to climb, removing all motivation. Social mobility, so visible across societies 50 years ago, has dwindled to a trickle.

This lack of financial education has put us in the dark, while steepening inequality has moved us to the edge of a cliff. We can't see if our next step will take us to safety or over the edge.

Just a little light might resolve that, helping us see which way to go.

That is the humble yet ambitious aim of this book, not to make you an instant expert in either zen or finance, but by taking a little of each, shine some light on areas that are dark, and provide guidance for some first small steps.

Hopefully that can provide a little certainty where there is stress. If it can help you see your next step away from the edge, and make that step, then it has done its job.

Seeing Emotions Directly

While I have worked in finance for almost two and a half decades, so there are some small corners of that industry in which I might be considered an expert, we won't be discussing those. They interest me financially and professionally; but I am not sure they interest anyone enough to read, let alone write, a book about them.

If it wasn't already obvious, I don't think about money with my eyes closed and saying "Om", and I didn't write this book in that state either. The desire to write this book comes from a few different times and emotions.

First came anger.

It started when I first began working in finance, with minimal background in it. After learning a few basic principles, like investments making compound returns, I couldn't believe that such simple, powerful ideas weren't being taught universally. To this day, I find it incomprehensible that our education system takes 12 or more years out of a child's life but omits teaching, properly, about money. I still feel that anger today. We have to do this better.

Then there was some compassion.

I regularly find myself impressed by low income and migrant workers, who are so urgently looking to improve their situation, moving themselves and their families away from the cliff edge. I am also in awe of the people who work to help them, and it was with the backing of a great team, of migrant workers and volunteers, that we produced *The Thousand Dollar Journal* for them, to teach some of the most basic, important financial lessons.

There was also fear.

After years of paying for their expensive private education, I realised my own daughters knew none of the lessons we were teaching to migrant workers. The fear that they might never unlearn their first bad lessons about money drove me to write *Happy Ever After: Financial Freedom Isn't a Fairytale* for them, as I didn't see anything else written exactly for them, or people like them. So far, it seems to be working (fingers crossed!).

Last, and perhaps not least, there was selfishness.

Having written a couple of books for other people, I wanted a book for me. One that I might have liked 30 years earlier, before entering finance, and might still enjoy today, that talks not just about money, but about how money intertwines with our life, our thoughts, our psychology, and how we can integrate our thinking about all of them.

Suppressing our emotions doesn't work. Accepting we have them, and then using them at the right time in the right way, does. Money doesn't have to be confusing, and it doesn't have to make you scared or anxious. It can sometimes be interesting, the potential it has can even be exciting and, used properly, could be the answer to some of your worries.

See it directly, as it is, and you can start the journey towards managing money properly.

Zen Money

A zen-like approach to money can help. If we see things clearly, we can learn how to manage our money better, so that we move our feet away from the edge of the cliff, learn to manage our stress, and feel better about our current situation as well as make better decisions to improve our future.

While some people temporarily search for peace of mind by avoiding distractions from the outside world, this often doesn't last long: the noise of life, and the demands it always makes on us, interrupt any peace we find.

Instead of denying this, we can try to take one of the noisiest, most distracting and frustrating elements of our daily life, money, and find the zen in it. This peace can last much longer.

There might be nothing in life that many of us see less clearly than money. We confuse it and the things it buys with love, status, respect, happiness and all kinds of other emotions that it does not possess. If we look at it through zen eyes, see it directly, we know that it is only us that has given it that power.

If instead we see it for what it really is, a tool we can use to create security and freedom, we can loosen the control it has over us, and we can use it to improve our lives. By using a combination of simple meditative and mindful exercises, aligning them with basic financial theories and practices, we can start finding peace of mind in our finances, not just when hiding from them.

Like an ensō drawing, we can find simplicity in complexity. Like the gold strands that fix the broken kintsugi pot, a thoughtful, mindful approach to money can be transformative.

And yes, zen.

Zen Exercise 1

On the next page is an ensō.

Please look at it.

Introduction

~

Humans Are Warm

We're more than just warm. We create our own warmth, and we can create our own happiness, joy, connection, pride, love and everything else that makes us feel like we are swelling with emotion. Bursting with it.

We can also create our own sadness, insecurity and depression, and all other emotions that make us feel like shrinking, curling up and retreating from everyone else.

We rarely do it deliberately. It's more often a reaction to the things we see outside us. Friends, loved ones, a favourite section of a TV show that we can recite line for line but still laugh along with all the same: these are all outside us, evoking but not actually creating the emotion.

It can feel like these emotions come from outside, but they don't. We do all this ourselves. We create them. They come from within.

Zen Exercise 2: Feel

Try this for yourself.

Please, do try it.

The last third of this book is full of practical exercises, and a few more on the way there, which if you skip over will mean you won't get the full value from this book, and we like to get full value!

Even if you did stop to look at the last ensō as I suggested for longer than you normally would have done, the other practices may take more effort, so it would be good to warm up.

Stop reading for just a minute and think about how you feel. Work through the sensations you have currently and try not to attach abstract nouns to the feelings, like "happy", "sad", or "neutral", but engage with the actual sensation, what your body feels like. Not just on the outside, but inside. Bubbly? Churning? Tightening? Loose? If you can't find the word, feel and remember the exact sensation.

Try to do the same for a time in the past, remembering how you felt at that specific time, whether elated, angry or depressed, remembering the actual sensations, whether it's a buzzing or fizzing in your tummy, a tightness in your head, a swirling in your chest.

Try it now.

That's it.

Thank you.

Money Is Cold

Money isn't cold as opposed to warm. It doesn't create any temperature or emotion of its own volition. It is just neutral. It is just a number. It just is.

It is trying to do its main jobs: help people move stuff around, and store stuff for later.

While it is being stored, it can also "grow". Of course, the money itself doesn't grow: it can't, it is just a number and a "1" can't become a bigger "1" just like a dollar bill in an envelope can't become two.

Instead, other people who want to use it to move stuff around need it and pay us for using it. They can borrow it from us, creating debt, paying us interest and eventually repay our capital. Or they can give us a slice of the enterprise that's moving stuff around, and we benefit as though we own it: equity.

Over time, those payments to the money we have stored attract more money, and those in turn more money, a process called compounding, and become much larger than we can imagine.

We may never be able to save all the money we need to be financially secure (although some people do), but the power of compounding over time can multiply the nominal value of money saved and invested over a typical working career by more than 30 times, enabling that person to be free from worrying about money much faster than they might have thought possible.

While it can do these amazing things, it doesn't have any emotions, and doesn't have the ability to convey any emotions. If you feel happy with money, the happiness didn't come from the money, it came from you.

Money Only Appears Complicated

When we talk about compounding, we've entered the realm where money can start to appear complicated. Too often we assume that all of it is as complicated as calculating the tax on stock options, whereas most of it is as simple as 2×2 (the starting point of compounding).

That's not how money is complicated. "We" are how money is complicated.

The complicated part of money is how we confuse it with the most important things in life. We attach price tags to the best of what life has to offer, like happiness, love, contentment, a sense of achievement, self-worth, and even peace of mind, when these don't need money from us. They can't take money from us.

We glue our emotion to money in ways that make us ignore what we really know. We then live our lives out of shape with what would bring us true happiness.

For so many of us, the pursuit of money to get these positive emotions into our lives can be the thing that keeps them away from us. Worrying about money can be the thing that keeps happiness out of our lives.

Think about the person who wants to be a millionaire, or to feel like a millionaire, so spends money on luxury items that wipes out their bank account every month, and so never comes close.

Think about the person who searches for peace of mind on far-flung beaches or in expensive exotic retreats, when their mind – and its potential for peace – was with them all along.

Think about the parent who so wanted the best for their child that they worked every hour they could, using up all their energy outside of the home, when what their child really wanted was the time and attention of that parent.

I hope you haven't been in any of those situations yourself, but I am sure you can relate to some of them or know someone who can.

Money Is Just a Tool

Money can be so simple.

The reality is that money doesn't create those emotions. It can't. There's no way for it do that, no connection between our wallet and our brain, gut, heart, or wherever you think your emotions live.

If you feel happy or sad staring at a piece of paper with numbers on it, or an app showing a balance or a chart, then it's you who has created those emotions, not the money, nor even the fiendish billionaire who created the app.

Money is just a tool. Unfortunately, it is not only one of the most powerful human inventions, but also the one tool we're given before we are taught to use it. As a result, in our relationship with money, we're like children running with scissors, wondering why we're constantly getting hurt.

Instead, at the most essential and simple level, if we learn how to use it, as a tool, it can help us live more fulfilled lives. If we don't waste it on things it can't do, like trying to buy happiness, we can use it to do the things it can: like helping us avoid or better handle the worst moments in our lives.

At a more developed level, we can build savings and investments that grow into more money, giving us more free time to experience the best things in life. We can make money work for us, instead of us working for money.

Zen Only Appears Simple

Even if I were a zen master, I know I would find it impossible to sum up zen in a lifetime, let alone in a book, or in a couple of lines in the introduction of a book. It is perhaps only because I am such a rank novice that I am even trying.

Evocations of zen through art might look simple, like the ensō circles in ink brush-strokes we are using throughout this book, but they are meant to represent something so complex that it is unknowable. By thinking deeply about the simple things, we can sense the complexity.

Zen *koans* work in the same way. We call them riddles, because that is what they are closest to in Western culture, but they aren't supposed to be solved. They are just supposed to be thought about, to help us think about complexity. They are there to bring us closer to understanding things that may be impossible to fully comprehend.

So much of zen thinking works on this kind of paradox: that through the simple, we can understand the complex. That through nothing, we can understand everything.

Buddha was proclaimed to have thought that his most important teaching was "Nothing whatsoever should be clung to," and it feels as though this statement can explain so much of zen's minimalist, non-clinging practice. It is the clinging, the wanting of something, that makes us unhappy: not the thing, nor even the lack of the thing.

Millenia later, recent research on happiness still probes into how our level of expectations is a main driver of our discontent. The secret to lasting happiness does not come through "more stuff" but less desires: the less we want, the happier we can be. If it is impossible to cling to nothing, less clinging equals more happiness.

Author Jodi Picoult once wrote that "Happiness is results over expectations", which looks to me very much like the following, even simpler, equation.

$$Happiness = Get/Want$$

Some very basic mathematics will tell us that we can become happier, increasing the happiness number in the equation above, by doing two things: we can increase "gets" to make the happiness number go up, or we can decrease wants.

Whenever we're presented with this kind of equation wanting a higher result (in this case happiness), we generally try everything we can to increase the first number, the amount of things we get. Even when we can't increase it any further, and know it, we keep on putting all our efforts into increasing that top number, without even thinking about whether we can change the bottom number.

The bizarre thing is that we do this, even though reducing the second number is more powerful. If you could reduce the second number to zero, the equation would equal infinity: anything divided by zero is infinity. There is no number of gets that can achieve the same outcome.

$$Infinite\ Happiness = Get/Zero\ Wants$$

Wanting nothing, clinging to nothing whatsoever, can lead to infinite happiness.

The emphasis on reducing what we want rather than what we get has another zen quality, in the sense of "seeing reality directly".

While instinctively we all think we can actually increase what we get, because it feels easier, it is reducing wants that is simpler, because it is the only one that relies solely on us.

What we get relies on other people: how much they will pay us, how much they want to charge us for their things, how much they want to give us, or like us. What we get is external to our control, no matter how much we convince ourselves of the importance of our hard work, our intelligence, our lucky charm, or star sign.

What we want, however, is entirely in our own heads. We are the only ones we need to tell.

As Epictetus, the Greek philosopher who had been born a slave, outlined in *The Discourses*, the chief task for a happy life is separating the things you can control from the things you can't, a sentiment repeated by the famous serenity prayer.

While it is arguably impossible to achieve zero wants (you would need to want nothing, which would then itself be a "want", hence the paradox that lies inside all great zen koans), just because infinite happiness might be impossible shouldn't discourage us from trying to achieve much more happiness by reducing wants.

The path to happiness goes through reduced wants, mindfulness and zen.

Wanting Nothing

Every morning at dawn, while mist still obscures the opposite bank of the powerful Mekong River, lines of saffron-robed monks parade through the streets and back alleys of Luang Prabang, receiving alms from the citizens of the town: sticky rice, some bread, sweets, enough food for their two meals a day. That is all they need.

In the past there were hundreds of monasteries in this magical Laotian town, one of the first UNESCO heritage sites, that seems almost too old-fashioned to remain in the modern world, a combination of archaic and even mystical. The town's architecture is a glittering array of temples, hundreds of years old, inlaid with gold and containing rare Buddha statues said to have been carried across the mountains from India almost a millennium ago.

There is still an impressive number of monks and novices walking through the streets in the last cool hour before the sun comes up, roughly ranked from older to younger, taller to shorter, with some stragglers at the end of each line almost comically tiny, mini-monks in their new robes that they regularly have to scoop off the floor. Yet despite their numbers, you can barely hear them, as they pad barefoot, silver bowls slung across their hips, in a cradle of their saffron sheet-like robes.

The town has become famous for this "procession", but this is not a show for tourists. It is a tradition that used to be practiced at monasteries across the Buddhism-influenced world, but Luang Prabang is one of the few places left on earth where monks leave the monasteries to collect their food in the morning. The closest the procession gets to stopping is when tourists take intrusive photographs.

The focus for tourists is always on the monks, but there must be an equally impressive number of almsgivers, as all the monks are fed every day. They kneel at the edge of the pavement on rattan mats, often in traditional woven costumes, with a collection of the food they wish to give to the monks in front of them. While tourists now swell their ranks, most are still local women, possibly mothers with sons of a similar age. They take a pinch between their fingers, whether of sticky rice or vegetable, and place it directly into the bowl of the monk in front of them.

No favouritism and no recognition is given on either side. The monks do not give thanks, nor do the almsgivers. It is surprisingly perfunctory. That might be because saying a hundred thank yous before breakfast is unnecessarily tiresome on both parties, but it is probably because all the locals understand how symbiotic the procession is.

The monks are thanking and blessing the people of the town. The town's people are thanking the monks for the blessings, and also for educating their children, as the monastery is often the place that young men in this poor country learn to read and write. The women might see their sons in the line-up, but if they don't, they know another mother is feeding theirs.

Whatever the motivation, the alms mean the monks have no need to work to earn money to spend. They spend their days meditating, learning and praying.

Infinite Financial Security

Just as wanting nothing, if it were possible, would result in infinite happiness, the need to spend nothing could result in infinite financial peace of mind.

Infinite Financial Happiness = Income/Zero Spending

Income is the money we get, after all. And we spend it on what we want. Income divided by spending is as close as we get in the real world to "get over want".

If we spend all our income, or even worse, more than our income, we will always have to work for more. We will never be able to save, and so will never be able to build wealth that will pay for our spending. We will find no financial peace of mind.

Except perhaps for the novice monks of Luang Prabang, it is not possible to want zero spending, but the path to financial peace of mind is just like the path to zen. Nirvana may be impossible to attain, but the path towards it is better than any other path. The path is faster, simpler, and clearer when achieved by wanting less, not by getting more.

There is, however, thanks to modern finance, a mathematical formula for enduring financial peace of mind, and it is similar in structure to the formulas for happiness and financial happiness.

You should be able to live on your investments forever when they equal 25 times your annual spending.

Financial Freedom = Investments = 25 × Spending

This is because we can withdraw 4% of our assets per year and they should, in most cases, last forever. We will explain this "4% rule" in more detail, and the path to get there – that is the path we discuss all through this book – but for now it is most noteworthy that the emphasis is on spending. Or not spending. The less you spend, the less assets you need and fortuitously, the faster you will save towards them.

The less you want, the happier you will be, and the faster you will be financially free.

A Simple Path to Financial Peace of Mind

The rest of this book is broken into just three chapters that we hope will help encourage you to move towards financial peace of mind.

The first, "Zen and the Art of Money Management" argues for how zen, mindfulness and seeing reality directly can be an important component of properly managing our money.

The second, called "The Path Is A MISSION" uses a structure from our previous book, *Happy Ever After*, to build financial understanding from the very start, money, through landmarks of saving and investing while suggesting methods to help speed us along the way. The idea is to see the path in full and know where we are going.

The third, "The Path Is Practice" offers 49 small and simple steps that build practical skills, add small nuggets of knowledge, and hopefully, most importantly, add to our self-awareness about how we are handling money.

If you read it from beginning to end, I hope it provides a path for approaching your money with greater certainty, as well as knowledge and habits that can help put you in a better financial condition, and a deeper understanding of it.

If you choose to come back to it, dip into it, I hope it can provide guidance when you need it. I hope there are ideas and practices you can come back to again and again. Even more, I hope it can move you towards a practice of managing your money. Understanding the theory of money is fine, but having a good practice is more important.

Here and Now

Perhaps the most zen idea of all to apply to money is the definition Alan Watts used in *The Way of Zen*, about how zen was a way of seeing the world as it is.

"It is simply a quiet awareness, without comment, of whatever happens to be here and now."

Until we start to see our engagement with the world as it really is, not how we feel it is or worry it might be, we can't hope for happiness. This is perhaps truer for money, and our interactions with it, than in any other sphere of life.

Chapter One
Zen and the Art of Money Management

~

No Judgement

Your money problems are not your fault. I know they can feel like your fault ("Who else spent the money?" you may want to ask), but you can't blame yourself if you don't understand something you have never been taught. Your uncertainty is understandable.

Engage honestly with how you feel about money, but don't talk yourself down unnecessarily.

Equally, while we learn more about how money can be wasted on expensive items, there is nothing wrong with buying things we enjoy. There is nothing wrong with taking delight in something truly beautiful, whether it is cheap or expensive.

No one here is judging you.

First, I literally can't see you. And second, judging doesn't help or inform anything. I have been where you are. I didn't enjoy being judged then, and it didn't help me. And it was mainly me doing the judging.

So don't judge yourself either. Any regrets you have about the past are at best pointless, and at worst turn into shame and denial that could block your path to peace of mind.

If we have never learnt to use a complex or powerful tool correctly, we know we shouldn't touch it. If we do try to use it, we don't generally blame ourselves for getting it wrong. Someone else who should have known better, or kept us away from it, generally gets the blame.

If we want to manage the money in our lives better, we need to understand this and believe it fully: money is just a tool.

By seeing money as it really is, we can downplay how much we think it makes us happy, or how much we think it makes us stressed, and have more of it to use for the things it really can do.

Being mindful about money, and our reactions to it, and not judging either, can enable us to be more mindful in our use of it, and manage it more effectively.

Judging ourselves, or imagining others judging us, has no place here. It won't help, and it will only add to our stress.

Zen Exercise 3

Do you know how you feel about money?

We may need to change some deep feelings we have about money, like shame or a fear of being judged, which if we don't address them, will hinder our progress along the path.

So, it is worth taking at least a few minutes to play a little exercise with our thoughts and emotions around money.

If you haven't done a free-writing sprint before, here are the rules: there aren't any. There are no rules, no right or wrong answers. You can give yourself a time limit (five minutes is good: long enough to write something, short enough to create some time pressure), but you can stop early or you can over-run. You can scribble fast, you can draw diagrams, you can loop arrows from one piece of text to another. As free as you like.

Easy, right? It should be fun too.

Write down on the left-hand side of a piece of paper "Rich" and "Poor" on the right, and then free associate around them. You can do this by writing quickly, if you like, without thinking too hard, and scribble, doodle, think on paper all around them. Then think about what you've written.

Or you can think about how the words make you feel, the physical sensations you have when looking at those words. How do your emotions react to them? They may be different if you imagine those words being about you rather than other people. "Rich me" and "Poor me" may evoke very different feelings from "Rich them" and "Poor them". Once you've felt that, write those down.

There are no points or answers here. Your answers are neither right nor wrong, better or worse than anyone else's. They just are. Look at them and acknowledge them, without arguing with them or reinforcing them. Now that you know they're there, just let them be.

The hardest enemies to fight are invisible ones. Just making them visible may remove the need for fighting. They may not need to be fought at all. They may not even exist.

Money Stress

The Playground

When you walk onto a trading floor, your brain may not recognise it as being the playground of your youth, but the emotions swirling in your gut will. There are no swings or chalk-marks on the floor, but the other threatening elements are there. People. Competitive people. Competitive people with minimal rules or supervision.

Cliques and gangs, bullies and the bullied, but all now occupying desks crammed with flashing screens, using language you don't understand, using it as code to keep themselves in and you out. Your stomach tightens an inch or two just imagining it on your way into work, wishing you were back on the two-week holiday that you paid for with the other 50 weeks of work.

But even if you never work on a trading floor – and wisely don't want to – the world of finance and investing brings that anxiety-inducing atmosphere to you, wherever you are.

The guy talking, no shouting, about investments on TV knows no doubt. He is always right, he says, if not in words, then in his posture. Another man who is also always right in his own head disagrees with him. As if this weren't enough noise, letters failing to form words are followed by numbers to two decimal places, and they march right-to-left across the bottom of your screen. It is supposed to make the boring seem exciting, so you watch more, but it only makes the unknown more nerve-wracking. There's no escaping the tension.

You seek answers and perhaps a little solace online – as though that has ever worked – but because the playground posturing can't be physically seen, it happens in words instead. In ALL CAPS. Perhaps every tweet or post by a "fin-bro" could be summarised: "Everyone not doing what I'm doing is stupid!"

And of course, you're not doing what he's doing. So you feel stupid. And stressed.

There are so many things to do. So many things to know. It feels as though it would be impossible to know them all, and that the noise would distract you from even some of them. Who can tell you where to start?

"It's ok," says the reassuringly upper class and well-dressed man, who represents a renowned global financial institution.

"I can take care of all of that for you," before presenting you with a stack of documents you need to read and sign, confirming that you have fully read and understood them, for which you would need the law degree you don't have.

"Of course he can take care of all of it for you," says your friend who knows about everything. "He's going to earn massive fees off you, directing you into products he makes more from than you do. You should do it all yourself."

You have come right back to the beginning, and the strands of stress have tangled into a knot in your stomach so fully formed it has a voice, and it says to you: "maybe I could just forget about this."

The Fairytale Trove

You step into the spangly warmth of the department store and are immediately welcomed by the lady who looks like your trendy unmarried aunt, who always had the latest clothes and best life.

Everything here sparkles, like a fairytale treasure trove. The cosmetics counters glow, the skincare displays gleam. You aren't supposed to know this, but it is because the lights have been set just so, bright mini-spots hidden out of view that make everything look as though it is on stage, on TV, on screen. Not real life. Better than real life.

Of course, we may already have seen these images in advertising sandwiched between, above, below or around the other content we want, featuring our favourite celebrity who wears the thing sold right there that makes her appear so perfect and so certain. Unlike our lives, the only ones we experience from inside, feeling all the doubts and problems.

Everything here is designed to make you want it. Everything you see, hear, smell, touch, and even taste, including the free samples in the food department, is designed to pull at the senses that connect directly to your emotions to make you feel it will make your life better. And yes, feel, not think, because this is all about emotions not cognitive thought.

"Designed" is the word too. None of this is left to chance. Psychologists have worked on every aspect of how we spend money to get more of it from us at every opportunity. If making a profit this year means making your emotions false promises, then so be it.

We all know from repeated experience that none of the things for sale in this shop will make our lives better for any extended period of time. If they did, and our lives are already better as a result, we wouldn't be back here, at this crack-den of consumption.

The buzz we get from buying might not even last until we've carried the bag out of the shop.

But we also know that we will feel sad, down, rejected or even slightly depressed if we walk away without the thing that particularly caught our eye. We'll have a slump in our shoulders and perhaps even a mildly throbbing head. Or worse.

We don't realise it, but we've just been bullied into doing something we didn't really want to do. Our immature playground emotions have been exploited again.

The Mis-education System

It used to be the case that the media images were in one world, on our TVs at home or inside magazines, while the desire to buy was marshalled into the store in town, but now they're bonded together, in our phones and screens.

One click.

The psychologists designing stores are no longer the world's leading experts at this. Now it is the people designing the apps who excite us, stimulate us and lead us towards the purchase decision. They learned the tricks from the people who made video games so addictive that players would spend days on them, hiring them all away so we would thumb-scroll down to the next message, post, item on sale.

We are all led continuously towards what they call the moment of truth. Do we say yes, and feel momentary minor elation, before forgetting about it? Or do we reject it, and feel bizarrely unworthy, impotent, unloved, rejected by the thing we rejected?

We have all done both. We all know how they feel.

The rapidly increasing difference these days is that there is no escaping this downward slide because we carry it with us everywhere. We have to. This is our contact with the world, with our families, our communities, our work, our pastimes, our reading, listening, viewing. We all have an excuse, and we all use all of them.

According to a shocking study by marketing research firm Yankelovich, we see between 3,000 and 5,000 marketing messages a day. If that doesn't seem possible to you, I am afraid that this isn't the shocking thing about the study: the shocking thing is that the study was conducted in 2007! Before social media. Before the smart phone. Before we carried marketing messages with us, interacting with people called "influencers" who, as their title suggests, are paid to influence us.

Marketing has become so constant, and the line between marketing and the rest of our lives so blurred, the study could probably not be done today. It would probably be easier to count the non-marketing messages. One – and this may be your only one today.

If information is designed to inform and educate us, the most prevalent education system on the planet today is marketing, educating us in the emotional importance of spending money. Almost nothing is fighting against that.

[12] THE LITTLE BOOK OF ZEN MONEY

You Don't Get What You Pay For

One of the most depressing but common opinions I hear when promoting saving and investing for a life free from worrying about money is people telling me that they "want to enjoy their lives now" and not worry about the future.

It sounds sensible, and in many ways, I agree. In most ways, in fact.

I want to enjoy my life now and not worry about the future too. That is precisely why I focus on enjoying my life and saving (and investing) my money. So hopefully I don't have to worry about the future and can enjoy my life now.

The depressing part, and the difference, is that the people who tell me this genuinely seem to believe that enjoying themselves now requires spending all their money immediately. Somehow, perhaps over-influenced by constant marketing with no resistance, they have tied money and enjoyment together so tightly that they now seem impossible to untangle.

No matter how much they earn, spending most, all, or even more than all of it, will be the only way they can acquire enjoyment – because that is how enjoyment is attained: it is bought from someone else, for money. They think spending money and happiness are the same thing. They think life equals spent money, as though they would only know if they had been happy in a month if their bank account was empty at the end of it.

It reminds me of gamblers who don't leave the casino until they have lost everything, even though they were perhaps ahead before, they stayed until it was all gone.

It feels almost too obvious to say this, but life is so much more than money. Enjoyment is so much more and can be attained for so much less. It is insane that so many of us conflate the two.

I believe that real enjoyment is often free. I don't want to say there's a negative relationship between money and fun (that's a lie: part of me desperately wants to say it, but it isn't true), I just don't see any relationship at all between the cost of something and the pleasure, fun, happiness or contentment it gives.

There is definitely a relationship between lack of money and unhappiness. The inability to afford something we desperately need can perhaps be one of the greatest causes of sorrow in our lives. There's no avoiding this, sadly. A flight ticket to see a sick relative is an obvious example. That's just another reason why saving money, to use on those occasions, is so important.

And then of course there is the slow burn of spending so much of our lives working for the money to acquire what we think we need, the time we could spend doing things we genuinely enjoy. There's definitely a relationship there. We need time to enjoy ourselves, so time spent away from doing that is clearly a bad thing.

But among our happiest times, money is rarely the most important factor.

Best Times

Think about your happiest times.

We will do another exercise in a minute, but first I'm going to show you how I did it. I promise you, as I was writing this, I stopped and did it myself, writing a list of my happiest times in a small notebook.

I wrote seven. Here they are in the exact order I thought of them.

First, because my mind was framed to think about things that didn't cost much (none of us can escape framing), I remembered a time I stayed in a beach hut on an island in the South China Sea for about $2 a night in the early 1990s. I remember thinking while I was there, watching yet another stunning sunset on the beach right in front of that hut, that I wasn't sure I should leave.

(If you've started making a list, take a quick look and see how many of them were similarly framed by your thinking before I asked you to make notes. Did you want to prove me wrong? Or right? Neither means you fail a test. It's more important just to observe that the framing exists.)

Next, I guiltily remembered playing with my kids in the park when they were young and crazy. "Guiltily" because we are also all framed to think that family and our children should be the thing that we think makes us happy, and I felt guilty I didn't go there first! But once I think about it, they were crazy, and there's no virus as infectious as the laugh of your child: how could that not have been top of my list?

Third, that reminded me of the scene I see so often now, when my wife and daughters are sitting around the living room laughing at something I just do not understand. At all. And they look at me like I am supposed to understand. It's still infectious.

Then, fourth, to be a little more selfish, I think about exercising, the trail run I plan to do later today with some friends. How while I might often not want to do it, the effects of it are so pleasurable. The ability to still run, move properly, can be the essence of enjoyment. Achievement, even.

That triggered me to think about achievement, a long-lasting sense of accomplishment. For me, that would include the charity race I organised, in Luang Prabang, that thanks to the amazing work of others helped fund a children's hospital. That still feels as good now as it did then, better even.

But then, sixth, my family jumps right back in again, and I remember family holidays, not just one but them all, the combined impact of them, whether on beaches, mountains, countryside, or city.

Last, there's time alone, like this, right now, sitting peacefully. While my family are still asleep, and I have made a simple black coffee and sat down to do some writing. Like this.

How much did these things cost? Some were free and some were cheap, but you would be right to point out that some, those family holidays for an obvious instance, were expensive.

Remember, my argument isn't that there's a negative relationship between spending and enjoyment, but that there is none. They don't all need to be free to make my point that there's no relationship between money and fun. The fact that there are free ones, cheap ones, middling ones and expensive memories all piled together shows there is no relationship at all.

Expensive Times

I then considered some of the most expensive things I've done or bought in my life. Things like the car that takes me to work, my children's school fees, my rent, a suit I bought but rarely wear now that we work from home more than we used to. A life and health insurance policy I've maintained for 20 years that (thankfully, fingers crossed) never had to claim from. And then there was a famous restaurant I went to where the food was interesting, but the bill just made me angry, so furious I could never think about it again without remembering the anger. Even now, I can't remember how the food tasted, but I remember to the dollar how much it cost and how that made me feel.

I can't claim scientific accuracy for either of these lists being "exactly" the most enjoyable or most expensive things of my life. They're just what occurred to me to write down. But that's not a bad indication, because if I didn't remember it, it couldn't have been that memorable.

Again, because I couldn't avoid framing this to discuss how there's no correlation between things I enjoy and things that cost money, I probably kept "family holidays" out of the expensive list, even though they've regularly been one of the more expensive items in my annual expenditure.

I could be more honest and include them, and it wouldn't detract from the argument. We aren't trying to establish that all the things we enjoy are free or cheap. We are trying to establish that many of them are. If enough enjoyable things are cheap, and enough expensive things aren't enjoyable, then there's no clear relationship between the two.

And it means we have the potential to spend our money differently to maximise our enjoyment and our finances.

If we drew this as a chart, we should end up with a scatter-plot that looks like a monkey was throwing darts at a wall. Wearing a blindfold. Maybe like this.

Fun

✖ Play
     ✖ Hut
✖ Laugh
          ✖ Race
✖ Peace
 +
Quiet ✖ Running

✖ Holidays

✖ Car

✖ School Fees

✖ Suit

✖ Insurance

✖ Restaurant

Expensive

This is my chart of enjoyable things and expensive things. There's a bunch of cheap to free things I love, a few expensive things I will admit I like, there's some medium-priced things I like a lot, some expensive things I am not at all bothered about – and that restaurant bill that I am still clearly not over yet.

Zen Exercise 4

If you weren't tempted to start already, please try this yourself now. Do it in four stages:

1. Write a list of your most enjoyable occasions or things.

2. Once you have got five, six, or seven of them, try to draw them on a chart, with how much fun they were

on the vertical axis, and how expensive they were going from left to right. Top right were expensive and fun, bottom left is cheap but dull. They should all, obviously, be near the top.

3. Write a list of your most expensive times or items.

4. Once you have written them down, repeat step 2. They should all be nearer the right than the left.

Please do it right now. Stop reading and do it. It will take a couple of minutes at most. My example is only mine. Yours will be much better as it will mean far more to you.

The pattern should be clear. Given the nature of the exercise, you shouldn't have drawn anything in the bottom left quadrant, because we were thinking about expensive and enjoyable things. Not cheap boring stuff.

If you have more expensive things in your "like" column than mine, that is fine.

There's nothing wrong with liking expensive things. It is only wrong to enjoy expensive things for the sole reason that they're expensive and not because they're enjoyable.

If we can recognise that there is no relationship between expense and enjoyment, we can focus our enjoyment on the less expensive side of our enjoyment chart and use that to save money that we might have wasted on the more expensive but less enjoyable quadrant of the chart. This is seeing reality more directly. It is being more zen about money.

It is even sometimes wrong to dislike expensive things.

Part of the journey that resulted in this book many years later involved me staying in the most expensive hotel I have ever stayed in. It was so expensive, I only stayed there because the money I paid for it went to a charity, which made me feel better about it: because the charity got all the money I paid, it made me feel less awful about spending that kind of money to sleep in a different bed for a couple of nights.

It didn't stop me wanting to dislike the hotel, though. I was so focused on the price the hotel regularly charged that part of my mind wanted to find any fault it could with it. I remember there being a delay between turning the tap and water coming out of the shower, and thinking how for the price they charge, the water should come out immediately. Yes, that ridiculous!

There's no point being that way, either. There's no point me still complaining about that expensive meal.

The only point is that if we want to save money, we don't have to look for joy solely in expensive things. There's lots of joy in other stuff, and we can redirect our searching there. And there is even more joy in the freedom that saved money can bring when it is invested, and bringing in an income of its own.

While you have pen and paper out, why not try writing out some other lists? In addition to the most enjoyable times and the most expensive things, you could try:

- A list of the things you use the most

- A list of the things you value the most

- Regrets – write down a few

- Your cheapest pleasures

- Your guilty pleasures (throw that list away before anyone knows you love crying during *The Notebook* and singing along to "Take That")

- Things you really feel you have missed out on – hopefully a short list

- Your saddest moments

They won't all be split between cheap and great, expensive and bad, but that's the point. To untie money and enjoyment we just have to know, and remind ourselves, that they aren't the same thing. You don't necessarily get what you pay for.

Fear of Missing Out

Once you have written out those lists, or at least thought about them, let's look at the last two.

Do you feel you have really missed out on an experience, or an event, or something that would have changed your life, because of money?

There might be something, but I doubt there are very many, and at least not nearly as many occasions we worried about missing out on at the time.

Scenario: Our friends are all meeting, and we can't afford to go. Our emotions are wracking our body, we feel so urgently we should be going, it will be amazing, there will never be another occasion like it. I will be such a loser for not going.

A week later, the event is completely forgotten. By everyone.

The fear of missing out "FOMO" sensation is almost entirely felt in the present about a future event, but hardly ever about a past event. Once it's done, it rarely seems to have been so important after all.

While some emotions can be long-lasting, like love, many others are short term. They will go away all on their own.

Money, however, stays, and by being invested, it can grow. We can spend it on something forgettable, or we can keep it and change our lives.

When we see life directly, as it is, this becomes easier to acknowledge. When we see money as it is, exactly what we should use it for, we can deploy it more effectively.

If you can recognise that the temporary fear of missing out is driving your decision making, and that you aren't really missing out if you don't spend the money, you are beginning to apply mindfulness to your money.

Avoiding Bad Times

Money can't buy good happiness, but it can help avoid sadness. Some of the worst times in our life could be avoided if we have money, and the lack of it can stretch them out, maybe even for the rest of our lives.

This could be something as simple as needing to pay for a treatment you can't afford, a visit to see a loved one, a need to work when a child needs you to be with them. That is really missing out. We should have a fear of that, as it is a feeling that will last for a long time, maybe our whole lives.

If you did draw the chart from earlier, with your high spending occasions or most expensive items, were there any you didn't particularly enjoy, where, if you had known, you could have kept the money to use for something more meaningful?

Think about moving money around on that chart, away from the places that it doesn't give us as much pleasure as free stuff, towards the places where it does. If you wish you could do that with past spending, don't dwell too much on that – just reflect that you can with future spending. It isn't too late.

Money Can Buy Happiness – On Average

There's a joke that Bill Gates (it hasn't been updated to Elon Musk, bizarrely) walks into a bar and makes everyone in the bar a billionaire – on average. It also hasn't got any funnier, I know, but the point of this joke isn't being funny, it is to learn something about averages.

They can do a crazy amount of levelling out. One outlying drinker in a bar, or one moment in a life, can swing the average up or down a massive amount. It's unlikely we will have one huge positive moment that can make an enormous amount of pain worth the suffering, but it is possible: it might explain why athletes work so unbelievably hard to win a gold medal.

Such extremes are unlikely for the rest of us. While we will undoubtedly have some amazing moments, we will also have some tough times. Money is unlikely to buy those best things while it will help us avoid some of the worst. That is how money can buy happiness – on average – if we use it for the things it can do, and not for the things it can't.

See it as it is, and it can do this.

See Money Directly

Money Is a Tool

Money is a tool none of us is taught to use properly.

This could seem arguable and unimportant, but it is neither. It is in fact hard to overstate the importance of this lack of teaching.

Money is one of the most ubiquitous, flexible and powerful tools in our lives, and so it is extremely dangerous not to teach people how to use it properly.

Consider just three uses of money, two good, one bad.

- Pricing a derivative option

- Effective allocation of donations to a charity

- Credit card debt to buy luxury goods

You might think the first two items are deliberately obscure, but they're not. Derivative pricing is one way of creating insurance (hedge funds initially got their name due to their strategy of "hedging" or insuring with derivatives), an important and powerful tool. Without insurance or hedging, entire industries could be so volatile as to perhaps be unmanageable, or too costly to scale up.

On a different spectrum, we can choose how to donate to charity by comparing how many lives our donation might save or improve. Most people follow their emotions with this, which isn't wrong, but the Effective Altruism movement tries to provide large-scale donors guidance on where and how their dollars might make the most difference to the world – which couldn't happen without money being used in the calculation. As a tool, it can and does save millions of lives.

And then there's the consumer credit industry and luxury goods companies which deploy decades-learnt psychological marketing techniques to put hundreds of millions of people on the wrong side of the compound interest equation.

You know which of the three you were taught. Perhaps not at school, but we all know which was the last one that sent us some information. I've never had a letter through my door offering me a free course on derivative pricing (a course I have actually done, if badly) nor have I ever seen a glossy advertisement for effective altruism. But my credit cards are my most regular correspondents, and I can't avoid ads for expensive things that will supposedly make me more attractive, or complete me. Good luck.

These are just three of the functions the money tool offers. There are countless others, too many to even begin to list, and so powerful that they drive most of our entire civilisation.

Compare that to a power saw, which we obviously wouldn't give to our children. Or a knife. Or even a pair of scissors we won't let our child touch if it hasn't got rounded edges, and plastic covering the blades.

But we give them money at Christmas. We connect money and love and happiness at the youngest, most influential age.

We understand instinctively that tools have power, that do jobs, that can be positive or negative – and that we must learn to use them. Screwdrivers. Hammers. Spanners. Wrenches. They all do the same thing, but not in the same way. We have to learn.

But because we don't learn that money is a tool, we don't learn to use it effectively. And we pass this lack of learning down to our kids in turn. We let them loose in the toolshed without the faintest idea of what's inside, because we don't know it ourselves.

Time and Energy

To understand what this tool is, we should start by looking at what it is made of. Not paper, gold or electrical signals in a computer, but money is made of time and energy.

I put time and energy into some money, or rather, to get some money from someone else, and I get some time and energy back when I give that money to someone else.

More correctly, perhaps we should say "give that money back", as historian Niall Ferguson points out in *The Ascent of Money: A Financial History of the World*, the first forms of money were normally debts, a record of borrowing and a promise to repay. The first evidence of money are versions of tally-sticks, a record of a debt that can be repaid with assets, that will themselves have been the result of time and energy.

Time and energy might seem to be abstract concepts, but they are the defining concepts of human life. Throw in imagination and creativity, more things that money can capture (we can be paid or pay for them), and we have so much of our life measured in it.

No wonder American writer Henry David Thoreau, who retreated from the outside world like a zen monk to write his classic *Walden*, wrote, "The cost of a thing is the amount of life which is required to be exchanged for it."

Here we have the power, and the danger, of money as a tool. It can measure, reflect, transfer, capture, and even store all human endeavour. It can transfer the good and the bad, the best and the worst, that we can do.

Any other tool you can think of, money can buy. Any tool you can invent, money can invest in the factory to build. Any capacity that humans have, money can measure, store, or transfer.

It can buy a gun, so it is as powerful as that. It can buy an MRI scanning machine, so it is as powerful as that. It can buy a book to teach people how to manage their money, so it is as powerful as hopefully that can be.

Nothing else can do this.

The Jungle Is Neutral

I had heard the following Shakespeare quote before, but it was burned into my memory when I heard it from Faith Spencer Chapman.

"There is nothing either good or bad but thinking makes it so."

—*William Shakespeare*

I met Faith on the beach at Pangkor Laut Resort in Malaysia in 1995. Around 70 years old at the time, she had swum a few hundred metres to shore after jumping off a boat in the middle of Pangkor Laut's stunning horseshoe bay, to feel close to what her husband had experienced almost exactly 50 years before.

Faith was the widow of Freddie Spencer Chapman, who was rescued from Japan-occupied Malaya, as it was then known, by submarine in that very same bay. On a pre-determined moonless night, Freddie swam out into the bay, treading water for what seemed an eternity until the submarine silently emerged and whisked him off to a hospital, where he met Faith.

He was being rescued after spending almost four years in the jungle behind enemy lines, helping to organise resistance activities. In that time, he was captured twice, shot twice, and contracted chronic malaria, blackwater fever, and pneumonia, spending 17 days in a coma at one point. In the jungle, not in a hospital.

The personal mantra that kept him going was that "the jungle is neutral", which later became the title of his enthralling book outlining those experiences. To him, this meant that his surroundings were outside his control, and he shouldn't expect them to be either good or bad, thereby keeping control of his mind, and strength, through the toughest of conditions.

Faith told me how she remembered Freddie quoting Shakespeare saying how only thinking made the outside world either good and bad, as she stood on the luxury yacht the hotel had provided to sail her to that bay. The boat was lovely, she thought, but this wasn't what her husband had experienced: how "bad" could the swim to shore be, if she didn't want it to be?

Without telling anyone, she jumped in.

Money Is Neutral

Money cannot reach inside us and make us happy.

This isn't a unique criticism of money, as nothing external can sustainably reach inside us and make us happy (some drugs can do it temporarily, different story). Our emotions come from within. Only thinking makes it so.

We all know it is true. At a purely physical level, we all know our emotions are internal and our circumstances are external, and there is no bridge.

While it may feel as though we have an internal fuel tank of emotional energy, whether happy, sad or more complex, there is no transfer mechanism between it and the outside world to get more happiness in. No filler pipe or fuel cap, no gas pump, no filling station.

Even if we know this, when we look around us it doesn't seem that other people believe it to be true. It appears that most other people's lives are driven by a connection between money and happiness, earning more to get more to feel more.

This is confusing inputs and outputs. Yes, the entire world is working to make money to make them happy. That's the input.

But no, it isn't working, because it can't. Nothing external can reach inside and do that, not money nor anything money can buy. Only we can do that. Only thinking.

Money Management

"We frequently walk with the sole purpose of getting from one place to another. But where are we in between? With every step, we can feel the miracle of walking on solid ground."

—*Thich Nhat Hanh, How to Walk*

The Simple Path

There is a reason it is useful to think of a path leading to financial peace of mind: one step comes after another. One fundamental concept and understanding of the nature of money follows another, enabling us to reach a destination, properly understanding all the things around it.

If you've ever been for a walk along a country track, you may have noticed how the route ahead is only possible to see from the path itself.

As a child, I spent many weekends walking, more colloquially called "rambling", in the beautiful hills near my home, called the Cotswolds, crossing field after field, climbing over the traditional dry-stone walls via styles or through farm gates.

Entering the field on the correct route, the path would often shimmer ahead across the field, the footsteps of previous ramblers evident in the blades of grass that bent just a little bit further downwards, and so reflected slightly more light off the sky back to our eyes.

The same path could be invisible if you came in via the wrong gate. From the side, those blades of grass are no longer reflecting anything back to you. They all look the same. The idea that they might do that seems like fantasy.

Even walking across the field, you would need to scan meticulously for the better trodden path. Only when right upon it would it be clear, and even then it might be too subtle to notice.

The same is true for all types of traditional paths, established only by practice and not tarmacked into modernity.

Walk along a woodland trail, and there will be slightly less vegetation on the forest floor ahead of you. Sometimes it will just be less growth on one side of a bush, an asymmetric shrub, that says you push through there. On a moonlit evening, a forest trail of slightly scuffed soil almost magically shines silver ahead of you, although it would be invisible from just a few steps to the side.

You feel like you might be imagining it, but you're not: the path is so much easier to see when you're on it, and you can stay on it more confidently.

While you could step on to the path at any point, you could also walk right across it, without ever knowing it is there. Only on the path, following the path, taking one step after another, is it obvious, and are you certain where you are headed.

Through a Complex World

If you ask people you know, or strangers on the internet, what are the first and most important parts of finance to learn, you will get a parade of different answers; from credit avoidance to tax efficiency, passive versus active investing, real estate, brokerage accounts, expensive fees, saving rates, interest rates, forecast return rates, legacy banks, challenger banks, robo-advisors.

You get the picture – if it were possible to get the picture of a totally confusing mess.

This isn't because people are trying to confuse us. It is tempting to feel that way, and it does sometimes happen, when companies layer hidden fees upon hidden fees, while telling us there are no fees, but most of the time that's not what's happening.

Even people speaking jargon-loaded sentences are rarely doing so to confuse the other person: they expect the listener to know the jargon too, as it is often just a short-hand way of saying something much longer.

When we learn a new concept that had previously been confusing, the "Aha" moment can quickly be followed with "Well, why didn't they just say that then. This isn't so complicated after all."

It's true. There are many more simple ideas in finance than complicated ones. The problem is, there are so many of them, because the world is complex.

Those two words are often used interchangeably, so it's worth addressing the simple difference: a complex thing is generally made up of lots of different parts, most of which will likely be very simple to understand; a complicated problem might not have many parts, but it will be difficult to understand.

Managing money is generally more complex than it is complicated. Each individual process is normally not too difficult to understand, but there can be choices around it, before it or after it, that make it much harder. Like a path, one step comes after another.

Each of us is different, and will need a slightly different product, whether it's a pension for a self-employed person or for someone working for a company. Everyone's situation is different, and each situation might need a different solution. Each solution might be simple, but the effect of adding all those simple things together becomes complex, and confusing.

Let's use insurance as an example: put very simply, it is a bet, and the insurance company is making the book. If you can place a bet on a favourite football team, or a horse in the most famous race of the year, and understand the terms in that race, you can understand insurance.

The only difference is, while you don't really care which horse wins, and so a winning bet is all positive upside for you, your insurance cover is against a thing you really don't want to lose. This can seem to make the sums less fun than the occasional flutter on a horse race, but it should make it more important.

A Burning Forest

We used to own a house overlooking the ocean in Margaret River, Western Australia. It was stunning. The first morning we stayed in it, I saw a whale breaching as I drank my coffee in the kitchen. A few years later we watched world champion Kelly Slater surf the big-wave "bombie" break in front of the house.

In addition to the breath-taking beauty of the area, the house was special because we designed it as a family to be exactly what we wanted. Every window, nook and cranny, was ours, designed by us for us. We spent almost every holiday there for 10 years, giving the kids a bit of wilderness away from their city lives, and us the peace of huge views and empty beaches, until it burned down in a bush fire.

We weren't there at the time and it is incredibly fortunate that no one was injured at all. Fortunate, and a huge debt to the local fire-fighters who risked their lives to fight the intense flames that destroyed more than 40 houses.

I used to think about bushfires whenever I was there. There were a couple of times when you could see the effect of one burning way beyond the horizon, looking at night like a strange angry sunset in the wrong place and at the wrong time.

Our house was across the road from a national park, with gum trees all around it. Gum trees can literally explode in a bushfire, sending fireballs huge distances in the wind, where they can start new fires.

That's exactly what happened to our house: a fireball flew over street after street, missing all the houses underneath it, until it landed on ours. Despite valiant efforts by the local services – the last picture we have of our house is a dramatic newspaper photograph of a helicopter water-bombing it – the house was lost, and the next time we saw it, all that was left was a tin roof, tortured by the heat into a twisted spiral, lying on a scorched pad of concrete.

Everyone was devastated, emotionally, but most people who lost their houses were financially devastated too. Nearly all of them were under-insured, and while the insurance companies and local authorities did their best to provide some relief funding, that was never going to cover the financial cost of rebuilding those lives.

While our misfortune didn't compare to theirs, as all we had lost was a holiday home, not our real family home, we were upset we had lost our house. We weren't, however, under-insured. If anything, we were over-insured. Not because we were clever, and other people weren't: a little bit of financial awareness meant we understood the nature of the insurance bet.

The following numbers are an approximate indication to give an example: the chances are maybe a thousand or two thousand to one any specific house in Australia burns down in a bushfire in a year. As a result, fire insurance on a $200,000 house would cost $100 to $200. What that implies is that insurers thought a house was likely to burn down in a thousand years, but it should last 500. There was no chance. It was surrounded by fire-bombs!

What do you do when you know your favourite team is going to win, and the bookmaker is offering wide odds? You double your bet. I took as much insurance as the company would offer me, worried that if indeed the house did burn down, building costs might by then have inflated, and the higher levels would cover me.

This isn't a story of how clever I am: the initial decision was my wife's. All I did was work out the probabilities behind it. Looking back from today, I cannot help but think how that small decision was life changing. That house was our single largest asset, and it literally went up in smoke.

We got lucky because I understood just enough about insurance to make that calculation. The people whose lives were ruined on that occasion and are ruined every single day by making an incorrect financial choice, were neither unintelligent nor careless.

They had probably accepted the minimum number offered to them by the insurance company, viewing it as a cost that could be minimised, and left it at that. Their education, which should prepare them for life, didn't tell them about this, how to calculate risk, or mitigate it accurately.

It left a huge gap, despite there being nothing in most elements of financial knowledge that a high school kid can't grasp.

This is why I sometimes get really angry about money not being taught in schools. This isn't a small thing. This isn't just about rich people or poor people or someone else. This is all of us. There are aspects in money that we all need to know, that can hit us from the side and ruin us. We all have these gaps.

Education Is a Path

Everything we do well today, we have learned, one fundamental step at a time.

We learned to walk, talk, run, read, sprint, write, one step at a time, one sound at a time, one fundamental at a time.

Before we could learn to walk, we had to learn to crawl, pulling ourselves forward with our arms, finally getting our bodies off the ground, tottering proudly around for a while before making the next step.

We see our parents or siblings standing, walking, running, and we instinctively follow, often literally, in their footsteps.

It's the same for talking. The bah-bah-bah babble that babies make is the verbal equivalent of crawling. That's them copying the sounds we make, without knowing what any of it means. And then slowly a few words start to sink in: "Mama", "Dada". In a year or two, they won't shut up!

If you try to learn a new language today, you will go through similar steps. You won't understand anything, your mouth will make strange sounds even you don't recognise. You will think you have got it right, and people will say it's wrong.

But slowly with perseverance, you learn, one or two little sounds or steps at a time.

Finance is probably the most valuable second language we can learn, after our mother tongue, particularly if we choose to measure value in money!

It is also, definitely, the simplest, with the least words and very little grammar, but you need to start at the beginning, with the fundamentals.

And small steps.

Begin with Small Steps

You don't learn a new language by trying to say "effective altruism" or "option pricing". You learn by saying bread, water, two more beers please, and thank you.

These are the kinds of simple words and phrases we might use every day. We need to learn how to talk to other people, so we learn the words for me and you. We need to ask for something, tell them something, and so we learn basic sentence structures that add in subjects, objects, verbs.

These are small steps. They are repeated by more small steps, one after another after another. This is what worked for us in our mother tongue, and it will be what worked for us in every other single thing we have ever learned to do. Step by step, we go on long journeys.

Small steps work for all kinds of reasons.

First, and most basically, when we don't know what we're doing they might be the only kinds of steps we are capable of making. We may not have the reach to do something bigger, so something smaller is the only thing in our reach.

That often isn't the case as we grow into adulthood and try to learn something new. We may have done similar things before, we may know people who do this, we may think it is simple just to copy them. We may have tried out a new skill before and taken big bold steps and felt it worked ok, so we are confident to try again. Until we go too far. Until a hamstring snaps. Until we lose money and don't know why.

Small fundamental steps are a way of avoiding that headlong rush into the Dunning-Kruger effect, best explained by British philosopher Bertrand Russell: "Those who feel certainty are stupid, and those with any imagination and understanding are filled with doubt and indecision." Simply put, ignorance builds over-confidence.

The key to over-confidence is in the "over" prefix: it leads to mistakes. There's nothing wrong with confidence, though, and that is perhaps what small steps do best. Build confidence, remove uncertainty, train muscle memory of the ability to conquer a small step.

One thing we all forget about learning is that there is a stage in the learning cycle where it is painful, where we feel stupid, and lost, before we acknowledge that we have more to learn, and become accomplished. Small steps lessen this pain, making it more bearable, but also enabling us to repeat the learning cycle faster and become used to the pain.

Some people are streak builders. They are good at doing things because they are doing them. Or they are bad at doing things because they aren't doing them.

Only small steps can build long streaks. Big steps will require too much effort to be anything but sporadically. Small steps are repeatable, either daily, or at the required interval, to become how we get to our destination.

The last reason small steps are the smart option is that we might not always know we are on the right path. To go back to the Cotswold hills of my childhood, those paths didn't always gleam across the field. Perhaps it had rained (it does that – that's why they're so green) or we had somehow come in through the wrong gate and couldn't see the path.

A little bit of uncertainty can be disorienting. You can spend ages looking at a map without it necessarily providing the answer, checking for landmarks that don't quite match what has been written down.

Or maybe you can see more than one path. Maybe the path splits in three, one going to each opposite corner of the field from the one through which you entered, and you don't know which one to choose. You don't know which is the right path for you.

A few small steps might give you the answer. A few paces into the field and the view may reveal itself: there's the church spire you couldn't see from behind the tree, and in front of it the gate you need to take out of this field. A couple of small steps will quickly help you find out if the path you are on is the right one. If it isn't, you haven't come so far that it is too much effort to go back to the beginning.

The Right Path for You

One reason for the complexity of the financial world, particularly as we view it from the outside world, is there are just so many different "things".

That's not because finance is complicated but because the world is complex, and finance is just adapting to suit what people want to do with their money.

There are as many unique problems as there are unique people on this planet. Individually, they may all be simple, but looked at together, or looked at by someone attempting to join that path, they look incredibly complicated.

It is also why some people who are financially secure and probably sufficiently financially educated for their own needs, tell you "What you need to do is . . ." and then that advice just won't be what you need to know. It might not resonate for you, or it might just be plain wrong.

This happens because everyone knows their own path better than they know the fundamentals of how to find a unique path. These comments are generally very well-intentioned, but each of us has our own path. Mine is not yours. Yours is not mine, nor is it theirs.

We all have different needs, different speeds, different styles. Any small thing, something even quite tiny, might mean we need to take a different path from our neighbour, or we may just be starting out in a very different place from someone else.

Luckily, there are some basic practices, some lessons and, to continue stretching the metaphor we have trodden down mercilessly so far, some landmarks to look out for along the way, to help us make sure we are on the right path for us.

Is It a Path or a MISSION?

Working with groups of migrant workers in Singapore, we arrived together at an acronym for the fundamental stepping-stones on the path from no financial awareness to knowing how to achieve financial security, true financial independence.

MISSION stands for Money, Income, Saving, Spending, Investing, Owning, Now.

This is the focus of the next section of the book, so I won't spoil it for you, but only by understanding money properly, can you understand why saving and investing matter so much. Only by saving, can you invest. And only by investing, can you really, truly "own" your financial life, one small step at a time.

There are no product recommendations and no stock tips, because all stock tips are wrong as soon as they are right (a zen koan if ever there was one), and we all need different recommendations for our specific situation.

Instead, we can learn how to walk, how to plan, how to look out to the future, how to read the landscape, and how to use the tools we need to get where we want to go. We won't always follow exactly in someone's footsteps, although we might at times. But we will know why and not follow blindly.

This will provide us with certainty, as much as it is possible to have.

It will also help us understand that there are things we can't be certain about, accept that, plan for that and manage it better.

How we walk along a path is as much about us as it is the path. If we see money directly, as it is, we can move towards an end goal where we worry about it less, in part because we may have enough, but also because we know how to get there, and what we shouldn't be worried about.

Don't Wobble

"Walk. Sit. Don't wobble."

—Zen proverb

I think in some ways this is the least zen saying, but in others the most.

It's direct, so I understand it immediately, which means it can't be very zen. When you're walking, just walk. When you're sitting, just sit. Don't wobble between things. Don't let your focus shift away from the thing you are doing. Be in the moment.

But despite this directness, it is zen: the direction may be simple, but following it is so hard.

Zen Exercise 5

Try to walk and just walk.

As late Zen Buddhist monk Thich Nhat Hanh describes in *How to Walk*:

"When you walk, arrive with every step. That is walking meditation. There's nothing else to it."

It's nearly impossible to think about nothing but walking. It is quite natural to ask yourself, "What even constitutes thinking about walking?" and "What does arriving with every step mean?"

It could be noticing the way your feet touch the ground, heel-to-toe; it could be the way your knees fold and extend, quite naturally; it could be your arms, swinging lightly by your side. The answer is yes.

It is simple but next to impossible. Perfectly zen. And like any good zen exercise it teaches us about what we are doing, how we live in a state of constant distraction.

Applied to our lives, this wobbling keeps us from accomplishment and contentment. Applied to our money, this wobbling keeps us distracted and out of control: we don't know why we spend and we don't know why we should save.

Save, don't wobble.

The Frame

Two things, traditionally, would be said to make Japanese art "zen". Obviously, the intention of the artist to make something that communicates zen ideas would probably be considered important. Something simple, perhaps, that conveys something more complex.

Second, we might be looking for something "wabi-sabi", that bitter-sweet Japanese construct of finding beauty in sadness, celebrating reality as opposed to impossible perfection, capturing impermanence, even loneliness. Nature, life, as it is, not how we want it to be, encouraging us to confront reality.

Translated very roughly, "wabi" can be said to mean loneliness, but also roughness, while "sabi" can mean old and impermanent. Lonely and old, rough and impermanent. This is wabi-sabi, and it is perhaps what we most commonly think of when we think of zen art.

We don't often think about the frame.

No, not the undoubtedly simple black wooden oblong in which our zen art is captured, nor the white mounted margins that makes all art look better, pulling our eye towards the picture.

I mean the edges of the picture, and therefore what the artist chose to include, and what they chose to leave out. The composition. How they chose what to depict, whether via ink, paint, woodblock, pottery, flowers or photography. They chose how much to put in. They chose what you shouldn't see too.

It could be a full cherry tree bursting like fireworks with blossoms, each one barely distinguishable from the next in the assault of colour. That's what artist Damien Hirst chose in one of his recent exhibitions.

Or it could be just a single branch, where we can pick out a few individual petals, seeing the delicacy with which their colours merge from pinks and yellows like a dawn sky, before fading into white at the edges. That was the choice of Katsushika Hokusai, the most famous woodblock artist of the Edo period, best known for his great wave images, painting one of the most beautiful sketches ever of an ugly branch with just scribbled hints of flowers at its edges.

The choice of composition is the artist's. They choose what goes inside the frame.

So can you. So should you.

The Podium

A famous and fascinating research experiment was conducted using footage of the Barcelona Olympics, which produced results we can all understand, despite them going against our natural first reactions.

Assessed by others, with no information than seeing their facial expressions, gold medal winners were deemed to be the happiest people immediately after their results and on the podium. No surprise there.

But they are closely followed by bronze, with silver medallists a distant third. On the podium of happiness, the silver and bronze medallists have swapped places.

We all know why.

The gold medallists, obviously, have achieved their dreams. They are the best in the world at their chosen endeavour (on that particular day, if no others).

The silver medallists can see one person between them and that now unachieved dream. They were so close and they may never come this close again. They feel out of the real spotlight. Silver medals, they may think, are for losers.

The bronze medallists see themselves one place away from the anonymity of no medal at all. They are on the podium. They are a winner.

And so it goes.

The person in fourth place is probably the least happy of all, distraught she has "nothing to show" for all the efforts of a life devoted to this goal, and got so close and yet so far.

The person in last place might be applauding all the medallists loudest, awed to be at the Olympics, part of this unique event that, let's face it, most of us don't dream of participating in.

And behind them, in the stand, a member of the crowd who luckily got a stadium seat in a ballot, is perhaps making their memory of a lifetime. They may never have attended an event this big before, feeling the roar of a crowd, and the unworldly balletic ability of all the competitors who are, compared to us, millimetres apart from each other in terms of talent.

In their hospital bed, a recovering patient perhaps feels that they are watching an Olympics on TV they thought they would never see. Every moment tastes double, feels double. They have won the gold medal of more life.

They feel it as it really is, more directly, more powerfully, more wonderfully than they have ever felt it before.

Each of these people is experiencing the same event at the same time, each through a different frame.

The Floating Buddha

The one obviously zen picture in my house is called "The Floating Buddha", a photograph taken as part of a series by German photographer Hans Georg Berger in Luang Prabang to commemorate the return of Theravada Buddhism to this magical little town, where it had so long been a part of the culture.

In the foreground of the square black and white photograph is a young novice monk, maybe only in his early teens or younger, head recently shaved, sitting eyes-closed, cross-legged, hands-in-lap, wrapped in monastery robes that drape off his body onto the forest floor.

Directly behind him is a rock, and further away, to the left, is another monk, sitting in the very same position, just behind a tree.

Strewn beneath and around them both, on the floor of the forest, are the huge leaves typical of tropical jungles, dried, curling at the edges, folding in on the veins and arteries that had previously been the thing that gave them life.

Because the photograph is black and white, the leaves are almost indistinguishable from the novice monk's robes, as if in his focused mind he has become one with the forest. The robes drape into folds and the leaves curl into rolls. They are merging together. His face is blank, as though calm in a rolling sea of leaves.

The monk behind him, blurred out of focus but distinct enough to see that he is older, bigger, seems to be caught in a brighter shaft of light through the trees, and appears to be very slightly above the leaves, floating.

I have loved this photograph since I first saw it. It was the innocent earnestness on the face of the boy, because he is still a boy, but looking for all the world like he has achieved a state of grace that I will never achieve in all my years. It was also the leaves and the robes becoming as one.

Only today, taking it down off the wall, forcing myself to look at it for five minutes, rolling the image around in my head, trying to focus my eyes on one spot and then another, steadily, but instead having to stop them zipping around from place to place, did I realise something. Or ask something:

> Is the monk at the back the floating Buddha? Or is the young novice in the foreground the floating Buddha, as he becomes one with the sea of leaves? I had always assumed it was the boy at the front, the subject of the picture getting the title, sitting in that floating Buddha cross-legged position, afloat in a sea of leaves.

But wouldn't it be more zen if it were the monk at the back, out of focus behind a tree, attaining the thing the novice in the front is trying so hard to do?

I honestly don't know, but today I noticed enough to ask the question. Today I got more value from the picture than I had got from it in the previous 8 years I have owned it.

Zen Exercise 6

Try what I just outlined. Find a picture. It could be a photograph, a painting or a drawing (but make sure it isn't on a connected electronic device). Look at it. Keep looking at it. Keep looking at it for longer than you think you need to, longer than you think I mean.

Explore it from edge to edge, corner to corner, what is in it, what is supposed to be in it. What might have been in it but the artist chose not to put in it. What did they put in it?

Are you seeing things you didn't previously see? Note them down, in your head or on a piece of paper, not on your phone or anything connected to potential distractions.

If there is something that makes it zen, about life, impermanence, then think about what it is. If there isn't, that's fine, you can inquire to yourself what it is about, what the artist's intention was when they composed the picture in this way. Ask yourself what they left out.

Please try it now.

Schrodinger's Observation

We discussed framing before, when talking about our happiest moments, and how I listed a couple of my favourite cheap moments because I couldn't escape the framing of wanting to show that enjoyable doesn't equal money.

It is difficult to avoid framing. What has come before this moment has to impact this moment in some way or other. It would be wrong if it didn't. It would mean no connection, no memory, no sense of achievement, no love. What is around this moment affects it too and should. Everything has a context.

But we don't have to be bound through emotions to our context or our history. We don't have to take the frame we are given: we can change it, we can move the borders. We can change the way we see the picture just by acknowledging that it has a frame, that it is a construct.

We can change the way we see our lives just by acknowledging that we are only seeing our lives in one particular way.

There's no need to force a change. Seeing what's there may well elicit the change we need.

In my probable misreading of Erwin Schrodinger's famous cat thought experiment, we don't know the nature of something until it is observed, and the very act of observation itself disturbs it. In his case, the cat was both alive and dead at the same time until he saw which one of the two it was.

In my case, I stopped listening when I heard that observation changes things. It is so similar to the nature of awareness.

Tara Brach offers a handy mnemonic in her mindfulness training: RAIN, with the R standing for "recognise". It could be "O" for observe, although it would mess with the acronym.

Recognise what is going on. See your emotions, your surroundings, your past, your reality, your perspective.

Before you observe it, it will continue to be in the state it is in. The cat could be alive or dead. You could feel frazzled, distracted, tired, hungry, dismayed.

Observing will change it. Even if you are still frazzled, distracted, tired, hungry or dismayed, you have seen this. You can recognise it, and by giving a name to it, it has already started to change.

Importantly, none of the letters in RAIN stand for "snap out of it", "change what you're doing", because those thoughts aren't necessary. Just seeing the frame will change it. When it isn't visible, it is invincible, because it can't be changed; it can only change itself. Just by seeing it, you have made it weaker.

A Better Frame

Any art looks better in a nicer frame with a big wide border.

The more expensive the art gallery wants to be, the less art they hang, turning their white walls into the widest borders they can muster. One solitary little print, spotlit in the centre of a blank expanse must be valuable, we think.

It might be tempting then to always seek out a better frame to make sure we're always at our best.

Yes, and no, said Tom Gilovich, one of the authors of the original Barcelona Olympics study. Having low expectations might stop us trying to achieve the goals that actually mean the most of us, just to protect ourselves from hurt. This will dampen everything: bad, yes, but good too.

Instead, Professor Gilovich suggests we, and athletes, can toggle between frames, to get the best out of ourselves and our situations.

Simone Biles gave the perfect demonstration of this, as faultlessly as she had performed throughout her gymnastic career, after deciding to withdraw from the team final at the 2020 Summer Olympics citing mental health reasons. Anyone immediately critical of that decision (no gymnasts were) should have looked at their own mental health when she came out to support her teammates the next day.

She must have been beyond distraught, but re-framed her position to understand that while she couldn't win gold for her team, she could still help her teammates win: and she seemed to find genuine pleasure at turning from the one supported into chief supporter. That is some powerful re-framing, and some strong mental health.

We don't need to perform such impressive mental gymnastics ourselves, and probably shouldn't frame our thinking about framing this way. It might be best left to the professionals, like gymnasts.

Instead, we will often just need to recognise and acknowledge that we are using a frame, and we will start to quickly see outside of it. This could be different perspectives; they could throw up different opportunities. We don't need to force ourselves to always choose a better frame, but just acknowledge that the frame is there.

Realising that we are seeing the world in a specific way is to start admitting that there are other ways to see it, and that it is not just how the world is.

A Clearer Picture

While we are looking at the picture, let's acknowledge what we're doing: we are seeing an interpretation of a thing, not the actual thing.

But then everything in life is an interpretation, our senses providing feedback to our brains, telling us what is visible, audible, tasty, hard, or smelly.

All our life is a selection of these observations because there are too many datapoints at any given time for us to comprehend, and so our mind frames a selection for us to choose from.

Our life is a selection of the thoughts interweaving these sensations, that are inspired by them or react to them, predict them or ignore them to think about the last sensation, or one from years ago. And there are so many of these thoughts, that only one at a time can emerge into our consciousness, selected by our mind as being the one to focus on, the thing in the frame.

This may seem confusing, although it is probably not even a glimpse at the real complexity of what is going on behind our eyes, it is a clearer picture of what we are doing when we look at what is inside the frame.

This is why it is so important to acknowledge the frame, and what is inside it. If we don't notice how we are observing things, what is influencing our interpretation of what we are observing, we won't have any idea of what the real picture is, of what our life is, and how we are choosing to react to it.

We won't know how much should be inside the frame for the picture to be perfect.

How Much Is Too Much?

If we don't choose the frame of our lives, it will be chosen for us.

This doesn't need to be as challenging as asking ourselves what our purpose is or searching for meaning in life: that is too much for a simple book about money.

If we keep the discussion to money, framing becomes more possible and understandable, because we can apply a number – and we should. How much is enough? How much is too much?

If we don't apply a number, the number will change all the time. Little by little it will grow, minute by minute, compounding and compounding.

It will change for good reasons, like inflation, where the cost of living has increased, so our number has to increase to buy the same lifestyle. It can need adjustment for other good reasons, that our needs have increased, that our circumstances have totally altered, or that modern life has moved on so strikingly, and our "number" needs to reflect that.

But it will change for very bad reasons too.

We should choose how much goes inside our frame, otherwise we will end up with too much that we don't want, and not enough of what we do.

"Maslow's StairMaster"

In 1943, Abraham Maslow proposed what has since become one of the most influential psychological concepts in his paper "A Theory of Human Motivation" for the journal *Psychological Review*.

He concocted what has typically since been re-drawn as a pyramid of five human needs, from basic to highest, that we are all deemed to climb in our lives.

Starting with physiological needs, like air, food, water and shelter, without which we can't live, we then move to our security needs, the requirement of being safe from harm.

Once these vital needs are met, we then move on to more "human" needs, the requirement of friends, interaction, being loved, and from there through into concerns of esteem, where we ask how we are viewed, both by the world and by ourselves.

Once these four levels have been met, Maslow argued that people can move into the final stage, which he termed "self-actualisation", or becoming the person we are meant to be.

While still too many people face famine, hunger and poverty, it is thankfully fewer than at most times in the past. The same is true of our safety needs too, with less people dying from violence in wars in the twentieth century than in any previous time, according to Stephen Pinker's data-laden book, *The Better Angels of Our Nature*.

(It needed to be data-laden because we all see more news about today than we read about the past, so we assume that life is worse, and will always stay bad. It isn't true.)

At no time in human history have so many people rushed up the lower stages of Maslow's pyramid, thanks not only to the miracles of modern medicine, but also to the outstretched arms of national education systems and the unseen arteries and capillaries of global infrastructure.

Many of us are almost born at level 3. Friends, love, community, belonging, perhaps with an eye already on level 4, status and esteem, being our prime concerns.

And here we climb on what I think of as "Maslow's StairMaster", which we have been mis-sold by generations of false advertising. Each attempt we make to take a step up in our esteem, the step moves downwards to the floor, and we are back where we began, requiring another step upward, and another, and another, and another. No matter how fast we climb, our foot goes down at the same pace, and we end up back where we began.

But unlike a real StairMaster, where this seemingly pointless activity would otherwise benefit our health, we get no fitter from Maslow's version. We receive no benefit at all. Spending on items that we think will buy happiness, love or status, we become poorer. When those things do not convey the contentment we had expected, instead of learning that this was a false construct, we buy more.

This trend goes by a number of names, from simple "lifestyle creep" describing how your standard of living expectations will imperceptibly inch forward, to "hedonic adaptation", suggesting that our happiness continually adapts to our current circumstances, regularly leaving us wanting more to be happier, even though once we have attained that "more", we are no happier, and once again look for more.

We end up with too much, despite the feeling of never having enough, or at least, not of the right things.

Torches of Freedom

Perhaps the worst accident to ever hit the human psyche was Sigmund Freud's nephew, Edward Bernays, starting work in the emerging industry of advertising in the 1920s.

Prior to this, advertising had been an industry focused mostly on the communication of information about a product, but through his uncle's work, Bernays saw human motivation as often being about different, more fundamental but potentially unmet, human needs.

And even if those needs were met, what if a nagging doubt could be exploited that they weren't?

In 1929, Bernays was hired by the American Tobacco Company to promote their cigarettes. In turn, he consulted psychoanalyst A. A. Brill, the first psychoanalyst to practice in America and the first translator of Freud's work into English, to understand why women didn't smoke, and how that could be turned around.

Together, they arrived at the idea that women didn't want to be seen smoking as it was deemed unladylike by men and other women. That was unlikely to change, so instead they pitched the idea that smoking in public was an assertion of women's independence, a movement that was gathering pace. If women didn't smoke, it was because they were being told not to, by men, and if not by specific men, then at least the patriarchy. With this frame, the products they sold were no longer just cigarettes, they were torches of freedom, like the one held by the statue of liberty.

The information was not about the product, and the appeal was not to meet a direct obvious need. The appeal was to a deeper psychological need, arguing that smoking would release them, which of course it didn't. It only reduced their wealth and their health.

And so began the advertising cycle of making an impossible promise only for it to be unfulfilled, requiring it to be met again, and again, and again.

Perhaps such basic ideas would not work today, but we now have an industry of torch-sellers, at every step of the way telling us we aren't enough, telling mothers they will be better if they use product X (if they don't, they are bad mothers, the world's supposedly most heinous crime), and telling all people they aren't successful if their possessions don't have a particular badge. Which will change next week.

How dangerous is this? At worst, the World Health Organisation estimates that more than 800,000 babies a year die in poor countries that wouldn't die if they were exclusively breast-fed instead of being given infant formula. And yet infant formula companies continue to advertise their products in poor countries as aspirational items for middle-class mums, supposedly unaware that many mothers in that country don't have a clean water supply, let alone sterilisation equipment.

At best, the advertising industry continually exaggerates an unmet need we may never have had in the first place, and when the product fails to meet that need (it's a car, not an ego extension), we feel more unfulfilled than before, and so look for the next thing, and the next.

Those middle three steps on Maslow's hierarchy, security, love, and esteem, become like a treadmill, receding away from us as soon as we think we have attained them. Everything we have been told that can fulfil our need for love, esteem, and even security, fails to do so, reducing the extent to which we feel it, and so we chase it again, and yet we never climb any higher.

As a result, many of us also don't fulfil one of the most basic security needs in level 2 – financial security – without which we will never quite feel as secure as we could, and so our esteem and status sits on even more precarious ground, requiring more topping up.

The Thumb Treadmill

I suspect we all experience a very similar sensation, at a micro-level, every day. The same quest for satisfaction, finding it, only subsequently realising it doesn't satisfy, and moving on to the next thing all the time, right there at the end of our arms.

Our phones are no longer our phones. They are questing devices where we search for the thing that is missing. Is it attention? We can check how many likes our last post received. Is it novelty? We can see if there are any new posts. Is it esteem in the community? We can see if there are any new posts that we can share that people will like? Is it moral certitude? We can see if someone has said something we disagree with, and argue with them. Is it aggrandisement? We can make someone else feel small.

Perhaps even worse than all of these is the quest for something we haven't named; an end to the temporary boredom we so often feel that itches inside our nervous system, in the back of our mind, down to our neck to our shoulder, along our triceps, inside our elbow to our hands, telling it the only scratch available is to pick up the phone.

Somewhere in the phone is the thing I am looking for. I can feel it now, asking me to pick it up. At this exact moment, as I am writing, it pops up a notification. It knows I need to be distracted, so it is magnifying the request.

It doesn't matter if it's an important email or a post about kittens, something in there will provide the distraction that scratches the itch. But only temporarily, and so we scroll again. And again, and again.

Each little morsel of information is enough to scratch the itch, but insufficient to make it go away. And so we scroll on. And on.

As someone who has experienced eczema for much of my life, the itch and scratch metaphor is not just a metaphor. That is what happens. You need to scratch; you deny yourself as long as you can, knowing it will do no good; finally you give in and scratch, and there is a searing burst of pleasure, a couple of seconds of sheer bliss and calm, before the itch comes back twice as bad as before. There is no scratching that will remove the itch.

While psychologist Professor Michael Eysenck first labelled the process of hedonic adaptation as the "hedonic treadmill" in Royal Holloway College in the University of London, I labelled this process, the endless searching for distraction, finding it, realising it hasn't worked, "the thumb treadmill", here, right now, at my desk.

It is the same. As we discussed before, the people who used to make shops the best psychological experiments in the world moved to computer gaming and from there to social media.

Each little bite is designed to be almost sufficient, but creates a taste for more, and so we scroll ever on, or rather down, looking for the thing that we've never found there before.

If scratching worked, eczema wouldn't exist. In fact, scratching is one of the things that makes eczema so bad: it makes the condition worse, not better.

Be the Experiment

I have once been a part of one of those research experiments myself. No, I wasn't given a marshmallow and promised another. Luckily, I was also never asked to torture a classmate.

My experiment was with my eczema. When I was 20 years old, it got so bad (the doctor took a photograph: never a good sign!) that I was sent to a research hospital in London that was studying a new project to see if it could help eczema sufferers deal with their condition.

From memory, I think the trial took four weeks. At the start, I was given a hand tally, a little metal device that rolled forward a wheel to show a new number count on every click of the button.

Week one was simple: I just had to click the button every time I touched the area of my skin with eczema, even the slightest touch, not just a full-on scratch, record the number at the end of the day, and start again the next day. The number was a shock, even for someone with an itch to scratch. I guessed the number would be in the low 100s, but it was over 1,000. Every day. Some days nearer 2,000.

Week two was a bit harder: try to reduce touching and scratching, but click when I did. It was hard, but there was a motivation to lower the numbers, and so they did come down. This was decades before "gamification" was a word, but give someone rules and a score, and they'll play the game.

In week three, we were asked to bring the numbers as close to zero as possible, and advised that if we really, really needed to do something, we could lightly pinch an area of skin near the eczema, but not so near as to disturb it. The numbers dropped down to a tiny fraction of the first week.

In week four, from memory, I think we were given a choice. We could try to maintain what we were doing with or without the clicker, but to continue to keep the numbers as low as possible.

I don't know what the "results" of the group study were, but I know what they were for me: my eczema was completely gone.

Anyone who hasn't had eczema won't know what that feels like, but at the end of week four, I met the researchers for the last time, and they explained the "miracle" I had just experienced. What I remember them telling me was the power of two key concepts that all other treatments, mainly creams and ointments, took away: awareness and agency.

We just aren't generally as aware of what we do as we think we are, and without tracking it, we don't know if that is true. Without knowing that I was touching my eczema a thousand times a day, I would never have known what cutting it back to single digits would actually feel like. I needed the awareness.

I also needed to feel that I was doing something about it. The agency that I could and that I was doing something about it was powerful.

In his 2018 book *Bullshit Jobs*, David Graeber quotes the work psychologist Karl Groos did in 1901 on the primary importance of agency, noting that even babies, before they can walk or talk, enjoy a sense of agency when they shake a rattle and it makes a noise. There's no point shaking a thing that doesn't make a noise, but once they know a rattle rattles, babies will smile or even laugh when their effort results in the noise: agency.

Agency is so primary that it is one of the first things that makes a baby smile.

With a treadmill for our thumbs at the end of our arms, we all need both of these. Awareness of the itch, and the agency of how not to scratch.

FIRE Worshippers

Empowered by similar awareness and agency, at the other end of the spectrum from people perpetually craving additional status items, are the followers of the FIRE movement, the initials standing for Financially Independent, Retire Early, and their prophets.

Reading their ideas, the zealous nature of the movement can be almost startling. While some proponents are open, gentle and inspiring, sharing with others their simple lives as suggestions for keeping them cheap, others have all the energy and certainty of a cult, knowing for sure that their way is the only way.

At times they can sound almost like John Cleese in the crowd from Monty Python's *Life of Brian*: "Burn the heretic! Kill the unbeliever!"

There may be some very good reasons for that certainty, though.

In this world where we are marketed to constantly, where the world's biggest and most valuable enterprises are designed to sell to us without pause, trying to get the very last dollar out of our purses or wallets, the FIRE movement has the missionary motivation to push back.

When it is done well (it isn't always kind, inclusive, or thoughtful, unfortunately, like many passionate movements), it does three things for its followers.

It alerts them to needing awareness of their patterns, tracking their spending, saving, and investing. They don't just leave things to chance. It gives them agency over their spending too, budgeting, planning, investing – all within their own power.

Perhaps more than both of those, though, it offers an answer to the big question, for how much is enough, an exit from the treadmill, a formula for financial freedom.

This is a very appealing thing – and not small. I can't think of any other philosophy or religion that has ever offered such a clear proposition to a prospective member. "Be good", "do unto your neighbour" are vague suggestions when compared to "save and invest 25× your spending".

Even more, the path leads to security and financial peace of mind in this life, not in an impossible to see after-life. That is the most concrete, understandable goal ever suggested: no wonder the followers are so devoted.

Unfortunately, that fervour can sometimes be off-putting to those outside, because they and only they know the answer, and that answer is a total change to our way of life. All you have to do is: "Stop spending any money as you have in the past and give it all to your new deity of investing in the index, where it will compound and bring untold riches."

The FIRE worshippers aren't wrong, the numbers do work, but the path they individually prescribe isn't and can't be for everyone.

What we need is a simpler path, a kinder path, but also a path we can understand well enough to make it our own. And we can start down that path by asking ourselves "How much is enough for us?"

How Much Is Enough

Enough Steps

Obviously, I can't answer "How much is enough?" for you. It's a hard enough question to answer for myself, and we all have different answers.

I have three ideas for you that may help.

First, asking yourself that question, "How much is enough?" could change the way you think. If you've never asked it before, or not asked it properly or often enough, this is the start of the change.

Just as Schrodinger knew nothing about his cat until he opened the lid of its box, we know nothing about the nature of what we want, about how much is enough, until we ask the question. Just asking the question is beginning the observation of how we think about this, if we have never thought about it before.

Ask yourself now, "How much would be enough?"

Because it is so hard to answer, we can tend to skip over it: "Oh, I don't know how much is enough right now, but one day I will know."

Immediately this tells us two things: we are reluctant to answer, and we are aware that our desires may change. We are tempted to think that we will be able to frame things better in the future than we can today. But we only improve at things if we start trying, and that only starts now.

Ask it again and try to answer: "How much is enough?"

This is not a question with a multiple-choice answer, or even any kind of a score. It could be high or low, but any answer at all will start the process of arriving at a final answer. You are making best guesses that will circle on an eventual result.

It could be like a painter, putting the first blob of colour on a blank canvas. Without that daub, there can be no painting. With it in place, the painting can grow into something beautiful around it.

We could ask, "How much would be enough right now?" to get a fixed point. That fixed point will be useful: like cutting a notch on a tree that we pass on our path, we can know where we were in the past.

It doesn't have to be a number. It can be a specific, a simple regular item of spending that we feel is a simple but bountiful luxury. For example, my wife sometimes points out to me that when we were first married, my opinion of a sufficient life was always having beer in the fridge and steak for dinner if we chose.

My life has in some ways moved on (I rarely eat meat or drink beer at home, for a start), but in other ways it hasn't, because I can still remember the sensation of thinking that yes, that would be enough. Having answered that question in at least one sense tells how far my life has moved on, and puts it into a context asking if all the ways it has moved on are good or bad.

Ask yourself that question now: "How much would be enough right now?"

Dig into the meaning you're using for the words, forcing yourself not to be lazy with choices.

Say these words in your head. "Enough? What does that mean for me?" Even if you can't answer, let those words roll around a little, so perhaps you will come back with an answer later. "What does enough mean to me?"

Imagine yourself in a situation where you know which of your spending avoids real problems, which creates real joy, and what you could do without, perhaps impressing others you don't really need to impress, or who aren't going to be impressed by your spending anyway (if they are impressed by spending, you shouldn't care about what they think).

Which one of those is more than enough?

Give it some real thought, and then condense it into something simple, like my beer and steak, that you will be able to remember. Write it down or tell a significant other. Just by asking the question and providing an answer, you are starting to shine light on a dark area.

Whatever the answer, you now have a better chance of finding it.

Second, if you can, try to calculate or estimate what an "enough" level of lifestyle would cost you a year. It's easier to start with monthly costs, and then multiply by 12. Rent, utilities, food. Maybe cheaper rent than your current luxurious apartment (maybe not). Maybe just basic food and not eating out.

But there should probably be treats in there too. When I set up my "beer and steak" baseline, those were the treats. I wasn't settling for them, I was aiming for them, so I have no place to tell the supposedly spendthrift millennial generation to go without their coffee or smashed avocado toast. Those sound like much healthier habits!

We want our lives to be joyful, and some of our spending will, as Marie Kondo so eloquently puts it, "spark joy". When we drew out our list of most enjoyable things, I am sure you noticed that some were cheap and some were expensive. When we drew out our most expensive items, the same. Some were amazing, some so-so.

It is ok to keep enjoyable spending, we just need to be mindful about it. I am sure you can already see where the zen comes in.

Total up this new fictitious budget: enough rent, enough utilities, enough food, enough joy. If this is less than your current income, you're in a great place. You can already cover the "enoughs".

If your income doesn't cover this, you're in a less great place, but it doesn't make the exercise any less important. In fact, it means you can extend it by asking two further questions.

First, you can check if your baseline is really more than enough, if any of those elements are still building in a level of luxury to which you have become accustomed but isn't really necessary. Or if any are the result of status or esteem pursuit, and if those actually work. Ask yourself some tough questions, and you'll get more insightful answers.

Second, whatever baseline you set, ask yourself if it is possible to stick to it, or at the very least remember it for future reference. This could be the line that if you cross it, you realise you're not really achieving anything, but are instead on a hedonic treadmill, and no longer really making progress.

Now take your annual spending number and multiply that by 25. Or your monthly number by 300 ($2,000 a month and $24,000 a year becomes $600,000, for example).

We will go into this in much more detail later, but that is the number that could bring you complete financial independence. It may seem like an incredibly large number, but remember we are artists putting the first dash of colour on a canvas. It won't look like anything yet. It can't, this is the beginning.

Lastly, imagine an emergency scenario. It could be an illness, or a zombie apocalypse, whatever makes it graphic for you. Use this scenario to imagine a level of spending that is genuinely basic, just for security, no distractions, no enjoyment, nothing. This is just living. It could be the rent that stops you living on the street, or the cheapest food that keeps you alive. The very, very smallest number that will enable you to survive.

Imagine a place you could live where the rent is much lower than your current payments (or the cost of buying a house is much lower), and how much the basic food and drink and power would cost there.

You can do two things with this number. Again, subtract it from your monthly income: the remainder is probably the most you could save given current income levels. It's good to know, because it frames our expectations.

Second, multiply this by 300. It will still be a big number (pretty much anything is a big number when multiplied by 300!), but it should be smaller than the first number. This is your financial security target: it might not be enough to retire on comfortably or play golf in 70s-style checked pants every day, sipping a martini in the clubhouse after, but it's way more important than that. If you can attain this, you will have a greater sense of your financial security.

These are your landmarks on the path to financial peace of mind.

Stepping Off the Chocolate Treadmill

Professor Eysenck's term "hedonic treadmill" describes how our happiness level always ends up back where we began even though we carry on chasing.

We mustn't be tempted into thinking this is a modern condition though. Jean-Jacques Rousseau described the same feeling in his 1754 *Discourse on Inequality*:

"These conveniences by becoming habitual had almost entirely ceased to be enjoyable, and at the same time degenerated into true needs. . . ."

With such a long history it can seem unavoidable, but there are some key clues in the terms used, plus recent research, to show how this hedonic treadmill is being caused, and how we can pull the plug out of the wall.

First, it is important that Professor Eysenck chose the Greek word "hedonic" to brand his treadmill, because the ancient Greeks, starting with Aristotle, believed there were two types of happiness: hedonia (or hedonism) and eudonia.

While hedonism is the pursuit of short-term happiness through any means possible, be it eating, drinking, shopping, with no regard for the future, eudonia is the longer-term happiness one gets from achievement, living a "good" life ("eu" is Greek for good, as in euphoria and Eurhythmics: sweet dreams indeed!).

When we have it, it sticks around for ages. It is an experience that the word "happiness" doesn't come close to invoking.

My friend Nick Thompson started doing beach clean-ups in Hong Kong during one of the first Covid-19 lockdown waves, and then began inviting others along. He told me the typical experience of people coming to their first clean-up, starting apprehensively, expecting it to be boring, but finishing both exhausted and elated.

He said, "They've been in the zone for two or three hours, doing work sufficiently easy you can do it for that long, but sufficiently strenuous it takes a toll. You can feel it. They've thought about nothing for hours except seeing a piece of plastic, picking it up, and putting it in the bag they're carrying. Again and again. They get into the zone, and when they come out of the zone, they know they've experienced something worthwhile. They're shattered but ecstatic. It's addictive."

The fact that the work is "doing good" magnifies that feeling even more. That's eudonia.

This doesn't mean we should only aim for eudonia and not hedonic pleasure though. A bite of chocolate is still a bite of chocolate – and we know this because of a wonderful study done by Jordi Quoidbatch of Harvard University and Elizabeth Dunn of the University of British Columbia in 2013.

They asked a group of volunteers to eat a piece of chocolate in a lab setting, and then come back a week later and eat another piece of chocolate. In between, the volunteers were randomly asked to eat as much chocolate as possible, no chocolate at all, or as a control, to do what they would normally do.

On their return, all subjects were asked how they felt after eating the piece of chocolate: those who abstained for the week (a whole week!) felt the happiest, and enjoyed the experience most.

Because hedonism doesn't last, it tends to produce a chase for more, until we don't really appreciate the more that we are getting. Managing access to the hedonic input, not getting as much as we can, is the answer.

This doesn't just work for chocolate. It works for everything. A period of abstinence, or even just change, will allow our bodies, mind, and emotions to adapt to the new environment before going back. It can re-set the base level. It can heighten pleasure and reduce pain.

We are adaptive animals: perhaps the ability to adapt is the greatest human trait, finding ways to live from the tropics to as near the frozen poles as possible.

Across so many human pursuits, using that adaptative capacity can be the key to progress. "Tabata" training, HIIT (high intensity interval training), or walk-breaks in marathon training all have research showing them to be more effective for improving fitness than steady, reliable, plodding workouts. The infamous "cheat day" in low-carb diets can re-set our body's metabolism when it is getting used to starving.

It even works for watching television, in a way that all of us will immediately think cannot be true: that we enjoy a show more if it has commercial breaks.

I know, right.

Every moment of our experience tells us that this isn't true. We hate commercials. We skip over them. We pay money to have them removed. We sit with our finger poised over the YouTube button saying that we can "Skip Ad in 5, 4, 3 . . ."

But a study by Leif Nelson, Tom Meyvis, and Jeff Galak published in the *Journal of Consumer Research* in 2009 established the opposite: that viewers' enjoyment of a show increased when there was advertising, in large part because the commercials put a break in the enjoyment, re-setting the base. Without the breaks, enjoyment levels slowly diminish, just as tiredness increases as we exercise, or as we run without a walk-break. It turns out that while we hate the ads, the breaks make us like the show more.

For happiness, removing the thing we are becoming used to, if only temporarily, can be so much more effective than looking for the next thing that will thrill us before we become used to it again. Stepping off the chocolate treadmill is far more effective, and enjoyable, than keeping on running on it.

This is who we are. This is how zen can help.

Maslow's Ensō

Maslow's hierarchy of needs and Eysenck's hedonic treadmill combine in my mind into two things. First, the Maslow's StairMaster we talked of above, the endless attempts to climb the hierarchy, without realising that our steps are taking us back down again.

But secondly, Maslow later added more gradations to the top layer of his pyramid, with the summit level of self-actualisation being "self-transcendence", where pleasure is not derived from hedonic pursuits, and one rises above daily concerns.

Not only is this starting to sound like "eudonia", the long-lasting happiness of living a good life, but it also to me implies coming full circle: that we have left behind the hedonic levels of the hierarchy of needs, where we endlessly chased esteem and status, and recognise the importance of the simple things. Food. Security. Love.

What if Maslow's hierarchy of needs wasn't a hierarchy at all, because at the top we realise that all we really need is at the bottom: food, freedom, financial independence to do what we want with our time?

If we re-drew the pyramid as a circle, going in order from food and security through love and status, self-actualisation wouldn't be a million steps away up an ever-steepening pyramid from our basic needs, they would be back right next to it.

It would start to look like that symbol of eternity that has been drawn since ancient times, from India to Greece, of a snake or dragon eating its own tail.

It would start to look like the most zen symbol of all, the brush stroke ensō circle, starting bold and strong, sweeping clockwise from six, looking like it is just about to run out of ink as it gets back to six again, before it re-starts the cycle.

Zen

"Try to pose for yourself this task: not to think of a white bear, and you will see that the cursed thing will come to mind every minute."

—*Fyodor Dostoevsky*, Winter Notes on Summer
Impressions, *1863*

Zen koans are impossible thought puzzles. They are designed to be impossible because the process of thinking about them, contemplating the impossibly complex, is more important than arriving at the answer.

The thought process is the purpose, not the answer. Probably the most famous modern parallel is the phrase, "the journey is the destination", which all of us have probably heard, but none of us ever contemplates while queueing for a seat on a budget airline flight.

The thought process is everything.

Scarcity

In his book *Winter Notes*, Dostoevsky tells of a teacher who gives every student in his class a bell, asking them to ring it whenever they think of a white bear – and then asks them not to think of a white bear. The bells never stop ringing.

In their 2013 book *Scarcity: Why Having Too Little Means So Much*, authors Sendhil Mullainathan and Eldar Shafir discuss how our minds are constantly trapped by Dostoevsky's white bear.

They tell how "poor" people are focused to the point of endless distraction on the things they are poor in, whether it is time, attention, money, or food.

They tell of an experiment in the Second World War that starved conscientious objectors (with their blessing) to see how best to nourish a starving population at the end of the war – and how the participants in the experiment became obsessed with food.

Anyone who has ever been on a diet will know how that feels. Anyone who has been deprived of spending on things they wanted will know how it feels to try to refuse a salesperson.

In modern psychology, Dostoevsky's white bear has been re-named "ironic process theory"; that way we just can't stop thinking about things we are supposed to not think about, and how trying to suppress the thought makes us even more likely to think about it.

Denial doesn't work. Denial builds frustration.

Focusing on the thing we are trying to go without will only make us want it more, and build a vicious cycle, not the virtuous zen circle we are looking for.

Living

In his 2018 book *How to Change Your Mind*, Michael Pollan discusses the ground-breaking work being done at Johns Hopkins University on the impact of a single psillocybin treatment to persuade smokers to quit: the initial experiments had an unprecedented 80% success rate.

The reason, according to participants, was that they had found so many other things to live for that smoking no longer seemed important. One quote rings out for me: "Why stop smoking? Because I found it irrelevant. Because other things had become so much more important."

This participant had found more to live for than their previous focus on smoking. Where all other treatments had failed, because they had required some form or other of denial, this treatment made it clear that he was in fact already denying himself a bigger, better life by smoking.

He had switched focus and may never think about the white bears again.

This is true for all paths to success. The path to success is not one of constantly denying ourselves the routes we wish to pursue, but seeing which is the better path, the one we really want.

The Zen Path

If we think zen is denial, it will not work.

If we don't want less, it will not be more. It will be less.

If we pursue something else, we won't think about the white bear, or smoking, or spending money, the thing we are "giving up", we will think about the other thing.

If we try to change paths without wanting to go down the new path, we will eventually find ourselves back on our old path.

Zen Exercise 7

On the next page is another ensō.

Look at it.

See if you can engage with it, think about it differently, see it more than you did the first one.

Chapter Two
The Path Is a MISSION

~

This second chapter provides a simple explanation of some key aspects of personal finance.

While the answers to many types of financial questions are specific to the person asking them – what stocks to invest in or how best to manage savings for tax efficiency – the key basic elements are the same for all of us.

We all have different paths. We all start in our own unique place and are heading to different destinations, but we need to use the same steps, the same landmarks, to arrive where we want.

Sometimes, it can just be enough to know what the right question is to ask yourself about each new stage.

I hope it does more than that too. By starting with fundamental theoretical steps, before moving towards each next more practical stage, we see each chapter as a stepping-stone, providing a route to greater understanding, not just of money, but how to take control of our lives.

A MISSION, if you will.

Initially devised as a lesson plan for a course on financial awareness and independence for migrant workers, the acronym MISSION (Money, Income, Saving, Spending, Investing, Owning, Now) provides steps on the pathway towards understanding money's real role and potential in our lives, particularly if we want to gain peace of mind from money.

We then used MISSION as the backbone for the book *Happy Ever After* to teach my daughter about money. If you would like a more detailed version of the MISSION, with some fairy tales about a slightly sarcastic, spoiled princess thrown in, then *Happy Ever After* is the book for you!

Rather than hiding from understanding money to achieve peace, we can use a better, simpler understanding of money to reduce our uncertainty.

While many of us spend so much time trying to earn more of it, and so little time considering how we fritter it away, immediately creating the need to earn more, understanding money can direct us along a much more purposeful path.

This isn't to say that money in itself is the purpose.

Money and the investments it makes can provide many types of freedom, and that is the purpose. That's the end goal of the MISSION. Freedom.

To start with, it can provide a freedom from financial insecurity, of not knowing if you can afford the next week or month of payments if something goes wrong. More savings and investments can provide a greater independence, an ability to decide life choices that might otherwise be ransomed to income levels. At the end of our MISSION, we aim for financial freedom, enough money never to have to work again (if we don't want to) and pursue whatever path we choose in life.

Once we know a path exists to financial freedom, the path itself can provide a freedom: a freedom of knowing the way. The freedom from feeling lost. The freedom from uncertainty, of not knowing whether we are supposed to spend to impress, to spend to entertain, to spend to escape, or just spend, spend, spend with no purpose at all. If we are on a MISSION, we know where we're going, and why, and that is in many ways the greatest freedom of all.

Our MISSION begins with understanding the nature of Money, a thing we think we all know, but don't think about deeply enough. We possess one of the world's most powerful tools, and we should know what it can do for us before we use it for other things.

We then discuss all the ways we can get money into our lives, income, before quickly moving to saving, the act of keeping that money: keeping the value we have earned, rather than giving it away to someone else, which is spending, the second S.

These first four steps of the MISSION should make us far more mindful of our day-to-day lives. Which is good, and missing for so many of us.

The next chapter, investing, is what will enable us to have greater control over our future lives by using another thing money can do: grow. It can earn money all on its own, and invested reasonably well, can earn more in our lifetimes than we can! Investing is itself the path to ownership, which is our O, and we need to contrast to debt, or liabilities, that reduce our ownership. And therefore our freedom.

And our MISSION finishes with N – for now. Because as zen teaches us, there is no other time. There is only this instant. If you want to start something, it has to be now.

From Money to Now

These concepts come in this order, because understanding each one is a vital underpinning to the following subject. It is hard to understand why we want income if we don't properly understand money, which most of us don't. We can't save without income though, so we need to understand that. And we shouldn't spend until we have saved, and we have to invest to own. Each step comes naturally after the other.

Like a path that you can only see when on it, the MISSION goes naturally from starting point to finishing point, through all relevant developments. While it might be tempting to jump in and start where we want, the fundamentals build real understanding, and the path becomes clearer.

These steps build towards a final goal of having enough wealth to give us far greater choice over what we do with our time: whether we choose to spend it working for more money, or whether we choose to do other things, things in which we may find more meaning or purpose.

And this is obviously why the acronym MISSION is so pleasing, as it conveys how taking control of our relationship with money and our behaviour with money can enable us to engage our lives with greater purpose.

Like any mission, learning how to interact with money can have a clear, important end goal or purpose – but it isn't the amount of money itself. The purpose of learning about money is to give you the freedom of thinking about money, to pursue the purpose you choose for your life, to steadily reduce or remove money worries, so that all you are left to worry about are the more important things.

Whatever they may be to you.

Start now.

The Money Step

It is always tempting to skip over the earliest part of a path, or a MISSION, assuming it is simple, just for beginners.

Too many discussions about finance skip over money, understanding what it is, what it can do for us – and what it can't. People who don't know this will spend their lives trying to force money to do what it can't, instead of directing it to what it can really achieve.

Money is a tool we use to record, transfer and store things of value that we or other people create with our time and our energy.

The record and transfer functions of money enable us to have far more efficient economies than we could ever have without them, swapping forms of energy from one person to another, one company to another, one country to another.

The store function of money is vital for our own lives, because we won't always have enough energy, or the time that it takes to produce the energy we need, so having it stored will be life changing. When we don't have time or energy, and we desperately need it – to help someone, or to help ourselves – it can achieve miracles.

This is what money can do.

What it cannot do is buy love, happiness, status, excitement, friends, joy, commitment, loyalty, compassion, connection, peace or even status.

It can buy peace of mind, but only if you know what that costs: if you don't, you can't buy it.

If we can direct our money from what it can't do, to what it can, we can have better lives.

Money Pots

It took what felt like hours of wandering around the Archeological Museum in Heraklion on the Greek island of Crete with my daughter before the penny dropped. "I get it. I actually finally get it," I might have said if there had been anyone else there.

My daughter wasn't there. She was rooms back, studying statues as diligently as someone should who is about to do a degree in classical Greek culture, and is just beginning a one-week dad–daughter holiday of Greece as a bit of a celebration. And she loves museums. Time was flying for her.

It was dragging for me, and I was desperate to find something to hold my attention. While there were some interesting things, statues and frescoes of bulls from the Minoan era (the legendary labyrinth of the Minotaur was said to be somewhere nearby), ancient helmets, a few gold coins, what there seemed to be much more of were shards of crockery, i.e., broken pots, with the occasional almost complete pot, stuck impressively together, even if it was with glue rather than the gold strands of Japanese kintsugi crockery.

There was no avoiding the pottery or avoiding learning about it.

The most bizarre pot, and one that at first glance seems as though the Greeks had got something hilariously wrong, was a type of vase called an amphora with a pointy bottom that would clearly never stand up. It felt as though the Greeks had experimented with pot making and not appreciated how important it might be for the pot to stand up. No wonder they were all broken.

Reading on, I discovered that these were deliberately pointy, and made for shipping, as the floor of the ships would have been covered in damp sand, and the amphora plunged into it: the pointier, the more stable, not wobblier. Genius, one has to admit, for a culture thousands of years old. The pots wouldn't move about at all, because they were pointy.

But there are so many of these pots: what were they shipping so much of that there are all these pots, or at least bits of them, left? Predominantly olive oil, but also things like honey, cheese, and other food products.

Ah, ok.

Energy. This was how energy produced in one part of the ancient world could be stored, kept safe, and shipped to another part of the ancient world. It was a container for energy.

Energy that couldn't be stored couldn't be used later, when it might be needed. There would be no advantage to creating a surplus, nothing to get through a weak harvest or a bad winter. The answer? Pots.

Energy that could be shipped could be used to buy different types of value, different forms of energy, ones that were lacking where you were. You might have olives but no feta cheese: no Greek salad for you. You might have meat, but no metal for making tools. You could have grain for bread but no grapes for wine.

All of these things are forms of energy, and they were all shipped: many of them in pots, that I now saw broken in front of me. Considering how long ago this was, and how few people there were in the ancient world, the scale of this trade compared to the size of the economy must have been enormous.

No wonder it was around this time and in this corner of the world, that King Croesus of Lydia is said to have invented money, a move so enormous that the phrase "as rich as Croesus" is still in use today.

And although many of us have started to increasingly use electronic versions of money these days, coins lasted much of the more than two and a half thousand years between us and Croesus, because money could do what pots could do, but better.

Life

We said before that money was a tool. To understand what this tool is, we should start by looking at what it is made of: money is made of time and energy.

I put time and energy into some money, or rather to get some money from someone else, and I get some time and energy back when I give that money to someone else.

Time and energy might seem to be abstract concepts, but they are defining parameters of human life. Throw in imagination and creativity, more things that money can capture (we can be paid or pay for either or both of them), and we have so much of our life measured in it.

As we noted before, Henry David Thoreau had seen in his seclusion that we really pay for things, and are paid in return, with our lives: "The cost of a thing is the amount of life which is required to be exchanged for it."

An amount of life means so much more than just time. Yes, we get the time they put into making the thing we buy. Often, much more valuably, we save the time it would have taken us to learn the skills they made this thing with. This may be much more than the time it took them.

A handbag. A coffee. A book. A laptop. The production processes of all these things stand on generations of time and labour-saving skills that would take us a lifetime or a thousand lifetimes to do ourselves.

Or we can hand over some money instead. Our money can buy us not just other people's time, but more of our own time that we then don't have to spend doing what they have done for us.

I will never be able to create even the simplest component of a computer, nor learn how to put any of those components together to function: I am barely capable of turning the router off and on again when the Wi-Fi isn't great! It's even unlikely I will ever learn to write any useful code, and yet I sit here, typing away at a laptop I own, that I bought with the payment for some labour I do understand, as though it is the most natural thing for me to do.

And so do we all, taking for granted our ability to switch something we understand for something we don't, and never will, and improve our lives immeasurably as a result. Our money saves us the energy someone else has put in. It can perhaps be 10 times more efficient than the energy we would have to use because of their innovation or their experience. Or 100 times. Or 1,000 times.

The thing we get might be 1,000 times more valuable than the thing we could make ourselves or take a thousandth of the time.

Money is a way of recognising all these things and helping us exchange them. It isn't a perfect way of exchanging them. It doesn't decide who captures the difference in value – it can't do that and that's a whole other conversation – but it does enable that difference in value to be created and shared by the people transacting.

That is what money does. That is seeing directly what is there.

It enables us to do this across the whole world, every second of every day, invisibly transacting with other people across the world, and sharing in the value we all create.

Store

Like pots, money doesn't just have to be used to exchange value. It can ship and store it too.

Imagine the time and energy we put into money is like electricity. Like cables, money enables us to move it from one place to another with very little loss, but it is also like a battery, enabling us to store it up for another time when we may need it more.

That time might just be later in the day, when we want some food, but it could also be later in the year, when we want a holiday, or later in our lives, when we want to stop using up what little energy we have left, and spend more of our time (and energy) enjoying ourselves.

The time and energy we convert into some money today might pay for a meal for us in 50 years. Invested well, it might buy you 10 meals, or a 100, or even 1,000!

The ability to store the time and energy value we create today for a time in the future when you may need it more is at the heart of financial security.

There's a saying:

Young people have time and energy but no money.

Working people have money and energy but no time.

Old people have money and time but no energy.

The sentiment of this can seem depressing, that at every stage something is lacking. Sadly, it is actually rather optimistic.

Many old people do not have money, because they didn't save it when they were younger, and as a result they also don't have much time, because they have to exchange it for money, doing so at an age where they have less energy, and so earning the money is even more painful.

Money saved successfully early enough could in fact result in having enough money to not work while still having the energy to enjoy it.

What Money Isn't

As important as knowing what money really is, it's important to address the things many people believe about money that just aren't true.

If we let these thoughts escape without attacking them head-on, they will persist at the back of our minds, and come back to haunt us.

- Money isn't love and it can't buy it.

- Money isn't happiness and it can't buy it.

- Money isn't any emotion, good or bad, and can't buy it.

- Money isn't respect or self-esteem or any other form of meaningful status, and while it looks like it can buy it, it can't.

- Money isn't the root of all evil either. How could it be? It doesn't have a brain, conscience, plan. It's just a few numbers.

Zen Money Exercise

Let's try an exercise, a free writing sprint. Please get a piece of paper and a pen ready. Don't do this on any kind of digital device – you'll get distracted, and it isn't the same. Get a pen and paper now before we go any further.

All you have to do is write down a prompt at the top of the page, and then write down everything that the prompt makes you think. Ready to go? If you want to use a timer, set it now, and write down "What money means to me is . . ."

And go.

Really, do it right now.

One of the keys to saving money is to get more value from the things we already own. Too often we buy something out of a sense of excitement that is relieving a momentary boredom, and then fail to get full value from it. And so we then buy something else, and something else, and endlessly repeat the cycle.

This is relevant right now because if you don't do this writing exercise, you may not do any of the other exercises that follow – and there are 54 more of them. You'll then have read what I hope has been an interesting book but failed to get a sense of the real power that you have right now to change your life.

If you do this exercise, you're getting way more value than the price of this book. It's the kind of exercise a coach would ask you to do, while charging at least 10× the cover price. If you're going to get better at managing your money, this is precisely the kind of exercise you need to do.

So, if you haven't already done it, do the exercise right now. This is your last chance. You know the prompt, and you know what to do: "What money means to me is . . ."

Once you're done, look at what you've written, scribbled and drawn. Separate some similar ideas, any themes that seem to repeat. You didn't have long, so there might not be that many.

- Did you write about feelings?

- Did you write about hopes?

- Did you write about past events?

- Did you write down anything that surprised you?

None of this is wrong, and if you feel like it, you can do this exercise again and again, adding to it, changing it, thinking about it more.

Use the answers like the first blob of paint on a canvas we talked about before. Smudge it, nudge it, add to it, move it around a bit. Play with it until it means more to you.

Your answers just are. It is better to see them than not.

The Income Step

While we have learnt that money is one of the most powerful tools that mankind has invented, we have also learned that it has an almost magical effect on us humans, making us do things we don't want to do, just so we can continue doing things we don't want to do. Zen philosopher Alan Watts referred to that exact process, very succinctly, as "stupid".

While the idealistic goal of zen might be to not need any money at all, and be infinitely wealthy as a result, the practical goal is to have enough money to use this tool wisely – for the things the tool does well – which we will start to learn about soon enough.

To do that, we have to get some money into our lives, ideally enough to do the things we want it to do. Income. We need money coming in. The challenge is to do that while minimising how much of our lives doing that disturbs.

Three Sources of Income

Although we now know what money can do, we should try to get some money before we spend it. Even if we decide to spend before we have earned any money, and take on debt, we will eventually have to pay it off, and we will need money for that (more money, in fact). Somehow, money needs to come into our lives, which is why it is called income.

Pretty simple so far. It would be nice to get it into our lives fast, and stop here.

Unfortunately, most of us are only vaguely taught about one way of getting money into our lives, if we are taught at all, when there are at least three:

- We can do work in a job for someone else who will pay us for that work.

- We can create our own job to do work for other people who will then pay us.

- We can invest money we have earned and saved previously, and other people will pay us for our investment.

While the last one is very obviously preferable, so much so that we will spend two of the next three chapters on saving and investing money, to explain exactly how that happens, it needs some money to start, so we have to work for it. Either for ourselves, or for someone else.

Working for Someone Else

Most people you know probably work for someone else, who then pays for that work.

As we noted when talking about money, some combination of their time, energy, and perhaps creativity or intelligence has been converted into money. The most common way this happens is that another person has an enterprise that has a need for those factors and will pay for them. It could be a private or a public enterprise, but whichever it is, someone needs those inputs enough to pay for them.

This is the most common solution to finding income for quite a few reasons.

One, it's because it's what we see around us. It's working in the nearby shop, or factory or school. It's available.

Two, for things we aren't taught formally, we generally have to learn by copying. This is true for things as basic as a baby learning to smile, but also language and work. Because working for others is what we see around us, and we aren't taught differently, it's the only thing we can copy.

Three, it's quick. Starting our own business requires us to do a huge range of things that involves, or that we worry it might involve, a business plan, incorporation, capital investments, getting an MBA, and so on.

It doesn't have to be that hard – really it doesn't – but when we need money, we tend to need it quickly, like air, so we often take the first example we see. Which is working for others.

There are a number of problems with this. The reality is that working for others is clearly only half of the solution to getting money into our lives when we have none. That's the first problem.

It's not a small problem either, considering that we get limited education on how to work for others, and none on how to work for ourselves. Our choices have been halved, if having only one choice left can be labelled as a choice.

Some professions really do teach the necessary skills in school or college, such as medicine (thankfully) and accountancy, but the rest of us emerge into the world of work with little or no idea how to do it. Most of us discover in the first week or so of real work how little we know, or how irrelevant what we have been taught is.

As for teaching us how to create a business, there are a few pioneering schools and courses out there, but it's nowhere near enough.

The third problem is that we probably won't be paid properly for our job: in terms of time and energy, we may put in a lot more than we get out of it, leading to a feeling of constant deficit. Even if we do get out as much energy as we put in, our time and energy may be creating much more value than we put in, but someone else may capture far more of the benefit. It could be the customer, the manager or the company owner.

It's unlikely to be us who gets more benefit than we put in, or we will probably get fired, the fourth big problem of working for someone else. This perpetual chance that our source of livelihood may stop, and then we'll have no way of buying more time and energy, for ourselves or our dependents, is another big reason so many of us feel financial stress.

Work for Yourself

The rising cult of the entrepreneur doesn't need another hype-man, and we won't do that for it – but setting up your own enterprise (let's not call it a business just yet) does have some clear advantages.

The first is how unlikely it is you are to get fired. As long as you're bringing some money in, you have one client in the world, you won't fire yourself. Similarly, you have a far greater degree of freedom over what you do: you don't have to show up to the office until you decide to show up, or not. You may not even have an office. You may just roll out of bed, check your phone, and start work. You may not even roll out of bed.

The ease of picking up an extra little business online in addition to your main job has led to side hustles becoming increasingly popular, often selling a range of products or services online. Doing this in addition to your main job has a range of advantages all its own, that you learn a new set of skills without risking everything. You might be able to build the beginning of a start-up by running a side-hustle in your spare time, or know why you don't want to; both invaluable lessons.

An additional income stream can also boost your saving and massively reduce the insecurity you might feel if your "day-job" ended, both valuable considerations.

When you work for someone else, you should be creating value for that enterprise: the enterprise then decides how to share that value, either with you, with the customer or with the shareholders of the company. In the last 40 years, the world saw a massive increase in the share received by the shareholders, and reduction in what employees received. If you run the business, you get to make that choice.

Lastly, working for yourself is likely to be the only chance you will ever have of doing your "dream job". Why would someone else know what your dream job is, and then create it for you? If you really want to enjoy what you do, it is more likely that you need to create that job for yourself. A side-gig might be your first try at that.

Work Stress

Unfortunately, most of us experience work stress, whether we work for ourselves or work for someone else. It comes in all kinds of ways for all kinds of reasons.

Sometimes it's as simple as being the latest thing in a list that we don't want to do, that we feel someone else should have done but is instead getting dumped on us, late, again.

Other times it's that feeling of cognitive over-load, that there are just too many complicated demands all at the same time, and our brain is starting to lock up. We can't see it, but inside our heads there's the equivalent of the spinning pinwheel on our computer screen to show that we need a reboot.

Or it can be the endless repetition of things we don't like, understand, want to do, with no end in sight, that causes us to feel like our lives should be so much more than just this.

And let's be 100% clear about this: it happens to entrepreneurs working for themselves as much as it does employees! You don't get money into your life without a client or two you don't like, and they're your new boss.

Do I have a magic way of avoiding this? Of course I don't, but I hope this book has a few ways of dealing with it. First, if it's possible, it shows that all is not lost and everything isn't hopeless.

Second, it does so in simple steps, so we can bite off little chunks. We might feel like we can't quit a job if we have zero savings, but what if we have five grand and a side-job we can do on the road? If that doesn't work for you, what would? Ask yourself that, and you're moving closer to it step by step.

And third, we are going to do so mindfully. Situations cause stress, but the emotions of stress also cause situations. The pulsing of cortisol through our system can fug up our nervous system from working properly, making the outside world seem worse than it is. A little bit of zen practice will help us see better what is really going on out there and assess whether our reaction or response will make it better or worse, for us and everyone else.

A 2019 article by the Harvard Medical School posted four coping strategies to deal with work stress: relaxation, mindfulness, problem solving, and learning to re-appraise negative thoughts.

All of those sound very zen.

Work Plan

The stressful nature of the work environment, even with the requirement to work from home (and perhaps even because of it), has pushed a continual stream of productivity tips, tricks and processes our way, telling us we'll be more efficient or effective if we do x, y, z.

These range from to do lists, work plans, standard operating procedures and manuals to little tomato icons that turn our internet browsers off after five minutes and apps on our phones that tell us if we're looking at too many apps on our phones (without looking, the answer is yes).

No. No more of those. Those are all designed to make your work more efficient for your company. We want to make it more efficient for you.

For that you need to turn some of those tools on yourself, and understand what it is you actually want, and how you go about getting it.

If you want to be able to quit work in 10, 15 or 20 years, you have to know what makes that possible (yes it is) and move towards it. That's later in the book.

If you want a side business that will enable you to focus on that and not your day job, you have to know it before you start doing it.

If you would just like a little extra safety buffer, to make you feel like you could survive a few months if your current job stopped – know that too.

Zen Income Exercise

Find the biggest piece of paper you have nearby. The back of some old A4 will do fine if you can grab that. Maybe get a few because you're going to be scribbling.

In the middle of the page, write the words "What does work mean to me?"

Now use a combination of the free writing exercise we did with Money, but this time in the form of a mind-map, with strands and bubbles flowing off that centre section.

Write whatever you feel. No rules. If you feel negative, let that all come out, until you have no more negative thoughts. If you feel positive or even ambitious, engage with that.

The goal is not to be right, it is to have something to look at and think about after.

Don't set a timer, just do it. Keep going until you can't think of any more and stop. Look at it. Think about it. There will be questions in there, useful questions to ask that you have never written down before, never acknowledged, even to yourself, so openly. There may even be answers. Try it.

If there are ideas in there that could evolve into a plan, separate them, put them into a list, and decide which ones you could do first. The best ones to start are small simple ones, but set a date to start.

The Saving Step

Saving always comes first.

When saving is a priority, every movement towards that goal will feel like success, boosting our mood and sense of achievement. It must be an action priority, with our saving money being separated from our spending money as soon as we receive it, to make sure it doesn't get mingled and spent.

If we do it last, it will always be as a result of denied spending, which will be stressful if we do it at all. Which we won't.

Saving Always Comes First

One of the most valuable fundamental changes you can make to your life is to repeat, understand, and follow this simple mantra: Saving always comes first.

There are three ways we can save money. First, last, not at all. Most of the world does one or other of the latter two, interchangeably, more often than not sliding into the third. Successful savers save first.

You might think there is no difference: "If I save $200 a month, it doesn't matter if the money comes out of my current account first or last". On the occasions that you do save exactly the same amount that you planned to save, then yes, there is no difference – to your bank account. But we all know that will be rare.

As we discussed in "How Much Is Too Much" in Chapter One, agency is one of the most important feelings underpinning human endeavour and satisfaction – and saving second isn't doing that. Just putting it first makes it the thing you are doing that month.

In the same way that both a yoga class or meditation session starts with "setting intention", a professional footballer thinks about where they want to kick the ball, or an athlete how fast they want to run or jump. The first thing they do is envisage what they're going to do, priming their minds and their muscles to do it. If they don't plan, it's luck. If you don't set an intention, it's not yoga or meditation – it's stretching and closing your eyes.

The intention creates the agency, which creates the possibility for success.

If, as soon as you are paid, you move a targeted amount of money into a separate account, where the money is either then "saved" or invested, that's the job done. You are then free to do what you want for the rest of the month.

If, at the end of the month, you have some left-over money to top up your savings, because you have been focused on spending less during the month, even better. You should do that – it would be amazing.

Done this way around, you have set an intention to save a specific amount, you have saved it, and when you got to the end of the month, you have either topped it up, or were able to reflect that you saved the correct amount.

Done the other way, putting money aside at the end of the month, you're not "saving": you just accidentally have some money left un-spent.

Not only does this lack the intentionality, it's harder (which is why it so often fails). All through the month, you will either have to think about whether any specific spending is going to take you away from your saving target. Or more likely, not think about it at all, and have no intentionality and no control. And then at the end of the month, there might be a sense of relief that you've managed it. Or not. You may have missed your target, have no money left, and feel a sense of despair that this is impossible.

Looked at like that, it's clear how much easier it is to save first. All we have to do is set up a regular transfer: if it's a repeat transaction, we may only have to do it once. A few clicks, and we'll be saving that much for the rest of our lives.

Look at what most successful savers do, and you'll know the answer. They save first. It is my favourite learning from the *Rich Dad Poor Dad* author, Robert Kiyosaki, of 'pay yourself first', because that's what saving really is.

It's a useful thought process, because it makes it clear that what we are paid by other people isn't ours until it is saved. Only our savings are what we are paying ourselves: any spending, on whatever it is, is what we are paying other people.

Pay yourself first. Save first.

The Predictability of Not Saving Second

In 1979, Daniel Kahneman and Amos Tversky noted a psychological trait called the "planning fallacy": people plan for things to be done much faster than they regularly take to be done. It doesn't matter what the task is, and it doesn't even seem to matter if you remind respondents that on previous occasions they have planned over-optimistically, they will plan optimistically again.

If you have always handed in your work late, you will predict handing it in early, but you will invariably once again hand it in late. No wonder it took a college professor to come up with this theory.

A fascinating study by Johanna Peetz and Roger Buehler in the September 2009 *Bulletin of Personality* showed there is a similar trait for saving money: a "budget fallacy". It not only showed that people spent more money than they planned to spend, but that there's a positive relationship between how significant it was to them to save, and their inevitable over-spending.

That's right. The more the respondents believed that saving was important, the more likely they were to under-predict their spending. They might want to spend less, and save more, but wanting just wasn't enough.

Reminding them of how much they had spent had no impact. Similarly to Kahneman's much earlier test, respondents were asked to calculate how much they had spent in the previous week before being asked to predict what they would spend this week. It didn't matter: even being reminded of their typical spending habits didn't stop them under-predicting what they would spend.

Perhaps more than any other reason, this is why saving has to come first. Instead of just planning or predicting how much we can save, actually saving it first instead will get it into the bank, and not leave it subject to inaccurate spending.

The Sound of One Hand Saving

Some financial awareness enthusiasts seem to be more enthusiastic about arguing with each other than they are about financial education and awareness.

It's one of the many reasons why the subject can be so confusing to outsiders, because there are so many opinions out there about what the most important thing is to do. Get ready for that. Everything we discuss in this book will have a counter opinion. How you can't be zen about money, or you can't be money about zen, about how you shouldn't invest this way, or you shouldn't do something else that way.

One of the most common arguments is over whether the answer to becoming wealthy lies in earning more money or instead in saving more money.

Income proponents will argue that cutting back on spending is too hard, and life will be unenjoyable if we don't spend, so focus on earning. You can always earn more money.

They'll post pictures of skeletons enjoying their retirement savings. They'll tell young people they'll be miserable without buying the things that make them happy (although that is perhaps not coincidentally often followed by a push to buy their online course for $500!).

Saving proponents are normally a little more reticent, and rarely selling something, but they take a side. They argue that earning more is only earning more. Too often additional income brings additional consumption with it, the dreaded horror of lifestyle creep, spending more as we earn more, without noticing any significant shift in our joy.

The debate is reminiscent of what is probably the best-known of all zen koans: "What is the sound of one hand clapping?"

As with all zen koans, the point isn't to find an answer, possibly because there isn't one. It is to engage with the question.

You can't save without income, so it's obviously necessary, but an increase in income without any saving achieves nothing. Both sides, taken on their own, don't achieve the end goal. The two sides of the debate are arguing for one hand's importance in making a clapping sound while barely recognising that both are needed.

Each hand needs the other.

There is one important difference between the two hands though.

Earning income requires someone else to pay us, whether it is the direct boss of the company we work for, or the customers and clients of the company we own. Therefore, at least partially, earning more money lies outside our control.

Saving money might feel like it relies on the outside world, and how much our lifestyle costs us, but many of the things we spend on are choices. They're our choices, which means we control them.

That's because saving money is an intrinsic activity, something we can do for ourselves and by ourselves, without relying on anyone else.

As the serenity prayer says, "Grant me the serenity to accept the things I cannot change, courage to change the things I can, and wisdom to know the difference".

Agency, the ability to effect change, is at the heart of happiness, but striving to change things we don't or can't control can be a key cause of frustration.

Earning more money is nice, and we can strive for it, but as we can't control it, we shouldn't pin all our hopes on it.

If we stop for a second and think what clapping actually looks like, it often looks like two hands moving, coming together in front of us. That might be the ideal, increasing our income and increasing our saving, cutting our spending, pulling both levers at the same time.

But it can happen with just one hand moving, as long as the other stays still. If on the occasions you earn more, and your spending stays still, you will save more. But if when your earnings are still, you will have to move your saving hand to clap.

Saving is something we can control more often than income, so it should be our focus. That's the hand we want to clap.

You Only Spend Once

Here's another thing that sounds like one of those old zen sayings, but isn't – at least not as far as I know.

You can only do two things with money.

Coming only a few pages after we discussed how money is one of the most powerful tools that humans ever invented, this might seem a little contradictory, but it is still true. Yes, money can buy anything a human can do, any machine they can make or any technology they invent, but that is just one of the things money can do: buy things.

We either do that, or save it. Those are the only two things we can do with money, we can save it or we can spend it.

We can keep it in our lives, for future use, or we can let it go, and it will never come back.

We can give it to someone else for something they have done, and that's it. That money, and everything it represents, everything we did to get it, the hours we worked, the energy we used up, all of which we will never get back, have also gone with the money. There is nothing we can do to get the money back, so we will immediately have to start putting more effort, more time and energy, into earning more.

Or we can keep it, save it for a rainy day, or any day, just not today. Because of the development of the financial sector, that doesn't mean we have to tuck the actual cash under a mattress. We can do thousands of things that ensure someone will give us our money back, and hopefully more. If we don't just save it, if we invest it well, it should become more money, and over a long period of time, much more money.

The beauty of keeping it is that we can keep it in lots of different ways, multiple times, over and over again. I can invest it in an index fund, sell the index fund to buy a single stock, and then sell the single stock to pay for a deposit on a house. As long as there's a strong chance of me getting my money back, or even more money back, then I haven't spent the money: I can use it later.

But once it's gone, it's gone.

The Profit Motive

In this way, savings are like the profit of a company.

If you ran a company, you'd probably want it to make a profit, for at least two reasons. First, if it didn't make a profit, you would never make any return on the capital or effort you put in. You also wouldn't be building up any more capital to invest in future growth, to take the business in a new direction if you want to, or see you through tough times.

In that way, savings are exactly like the profit of a company. It is the capital you build up to do any number of things. It could see you through tough times personally. It could buy new assets that change your life immeasurably.

Spending all the money is making no profit. Saving is making a profit, having money to invest in the future.

Second, very few companies, not even "non-profits" or "not-for-profits" make "zero-profits". Think about it: that would be next to impossible, to have exactly the same income as you have expenses, to the cent. It is much more likely you will have more or less.

And if you don't plan to have more income than expenses, and save it first, it is much, much, much more likely you will have less. This will lead to losses, debt, and bankruptcy.

Aiming for profit, for savings, gives you a chance of avoiding this. Not aiming makes it entirely luck – and that's not saving. It's luck.

Motivation

You might not be the kind of person who wants to think about making a profit, but that's only the first half of the phrase "profit motive". The second part is even more important: motivation.

If you understand the importance of saving, of building a financial buffer for the rest of your life, that can provide security, peace of mind or even freedom, you have to recognise that motivation in your daily life.

The motivation to save will make this enjoyable. The movement towards a saving target will turn any progress you make an achievement, something to be proud of and enjoy.

Author of *How to Change The World*, John-Paul Flintoff, gives a wonderful and simple example of how setting intentionality, and motivation, can change our perspective on everything we do.

He uses the example of taking a friend's dog for a walk when the friend is too sick to do so. If we view this as a chore, every moment of the walk will be a pain, a drag, a bore. We will wish we were doing something else instead.

If we view this as something we are doing to help someone else, because we are a good person, helping to make the world a better place, if only in a small way, it will be a delight to do. The joy of doing it will stretch on for long after the walk, as we will physically and emotionally feel a sense of accomplishment and warmth from it that we can tap back into at any point.

In my mind's eye, I can even see the sun is shining on one of those walks, and not on the other! That is the power of motivation.

This sense of motivation is vital for saving, because saving must not just be the denial of spending desires. If it is, it will be that dog-walk in the rain, the dog will have diarrhoea and we will have run out of plastic bags. And we'll be doing it every single day.

Saving must not be what we have left over after we've spent what we want. Instead, it must take us towards a saving target, and each coin, note, and digital number saved in our account moves us towards those targets.

What Are We Saving For?

I think of saving as having three different levels as targets.

- Your first target is to have enough money to cover an emergency (if you have no savings or debt, this is your level).

- The second target is to have enough money to start investing.

- The third is to build that fund to the point it can pay for you never to need to work again – 25× your annual spending.

That first target is crucial for financial peace of mind – and security. In late 2019, 61% of Americans did not have $1,000 saved for an emergency, according to a Bank Rate survey, before we all got hit with the biggest emergency most of us had ever experienced.

Many people will tell you $1,000 isn't a big enough emergency fund, and while they're right, they are missing the vital point that it is a whole thousand dollars better than nothing. In many ways, it is the most important amount of money to have saved, because it will stop even small emergencies, needing $500 in a crunch, to repair a car or pay an unexpected bill, from turning into a crisis that needs you to take on debt, that can then spiral into more and more debt.

If you don't have $1,000 (or pounds, or euros) saved, this is your first target. This could save your life.

That first grand is also the most important because it will show you that you can do it. If you can save this much, you can do it again, and save for a bigger emergency fund – perhaps up to the recommended scale of three months of your basic spending level. This will mean you can not only cover an unexpected cost, you can also cover an equally unexpected loss of work, for whatever reason it happens.

Reflect on this. This is a peace of mind that you can't have when living hand-to-mouth, paycheck to paycheck. If something went wrong, an illness, a need to move, an economic crisis, another pandemic – you could survive for at least three months.

Those are some real-life concerns you can now stop worrying about. If you didn't worry about them before you had the money, no doubt they were there – you might just have been in denial. Now they are gone: you have cover.

With an emergency properly funded, you are then saving to invest. We will discuss this more in a couple of chapters' time, but the difference here is that your emergency fund probably shouldn't be in very high risk/high return investments, while your investment fund might be, so it can make higher returns and grow faster.

Every time your investment fund does grow, your financial security is increasing: it can pay for more and more months of your basic living, meaning that maybe you could stop work for a whole year, or two.

Or forever. Once your investment fund has reached twenty-five times your monthly spending, yes, you can stop working forever.

This seems a long way off, I know, but it is the end of the path. Some people will be able to skip and run along the path all the way to its destination with no problems at all. Others of us will trudge and hike, get caught in mud, and occasionally even be worried we have completely lost the path, or doubled back on ourselves.

But the path is there, and we move along it by saving, regularly, successfully, as a priority. If we move along the path with intentional goals in mind, acknowledging when we achieve those goals, that progress itself can boost our peace of mind, in addition to the money.

Two Steps: A Tiny One and Half Again

More than anything else, the habit of saving money first is the most important. Put some money aside, no matter how tiny, right now. Really, no amount is too small to start. Just separate some money from your spending, and get it to a new account where you can't spend it, and where you can earn a return on it.

Keep doing that and you will be better off than you were before. Keep doing that and you will probably find occasions when you can save more, when you want to grow your savings faster. Successful savers see their totals become a goal that is more important than their spending – and it starts with the habit of saving first.

Second, target saving half of any increase you get in income. Not all of it, which will be too painful, and not none of it, as then you will get used to the spending. Target half of any increase, and you will see your savings growth steadily accelerate over time.

These two steps, small, simple but psychologically supportive, can get you on top of your savings, even from a very low income level.

Zen Saving Exercise

Let's make this an easy exercise. No writing or drawing required this time. Let's just close our eyes and think about what having no financial worries would feel like.

We don't want to imagine riches, a super-yacht, endless holidays, a garden party with glamorous friends: that's daydreaming.

Instead, consider what having enough money not to worry about it would mean to you. You might need to think about the opposite first: what your money worries feel like, what the physical sensations of stress are.

Then imagine them gone. Try it now.

The Spending Step

"Let go or be dragged."

—*Traditional*

We can't avoid spending, but that doesn't mean we should avoid thinking about it. To gain financial peace of mind, we have to take control of our money, and that means taking control of our spending. That means looking it in the eye, knowing with aware minds and full open hearts how we are spending, and how this is moving us towards, or away from, a better life.

Spending less will increase our savings, improving our futures, while spending better will improve our lives today. Only by knowing what we spend can we do either.

Take note. Write down your spending.

Not All Spending Is Bad

Now we have said that "saving always comes first" we can be clear about something else: it is ok for spending to come second. Spending is necessary, and that isn't supposed to imply that it's a necessary evil. Spending is a necessary good. By spending money, we can bring wonderful things into our lives that we would never otherwise be able to get. It can be life-changing. It can be amazing.

We just need to know where it sits in our priorities and if that is helping us.

When you drew your chart of your happiest moments, I bet some of them involved spending some money. Maybe even all of them.

As we said at the time, the point wasn't to show that spending money couldn't have a positive impact on our lives – but to show that spending all of it wouldn't always bring about maximum results.

If we want to optimise our lives, the chances are that we are going to need to spend money.

Saying "saving always comes first" reflects the importance of saving, reversing the order of so much of what we see around us, that encourages us to spend. Saving first means we immediately reduce our worries about financial insecurity, one of the things money can really do, freeing up our thinking about spending.

But how much should we spend?

But Spending It All Might Be

If we remember the monks of Luang Prabang, collecting all the food they needed for the day from local people (and a few tourists), they spent no money at all.

Imagine if that were possible for the rest of us. If we didn't need to spend any money at all, we wouldn't need to work at all. All our lives would be free to do whatever we want to do.

If we could live off the land, picking blackberries from hedgerow brambles, scrumping apples from the local orchard, and taking beautiful social media–worthy pictures of them both with phones and data that we somehow managed to acquire in a similarly free manner.

Yes, the rest of our lives are very far from those idyllic Lao monks.

Instead, the majority of the world, which includes you and me, has to spend money to get even the very basic things they want.

But then once we've earned it, and started spending it, we don't know where we should stop. No one has told us, "stop spending at this amount" except for the very obvious but even more vague "within your means".

Let's assume we do live within our means, and don't borrow to live. If we spend all our money, we will always need to work to live. We will build no savings that can earn income on our behalf to pay for any time we don't want to work but still need to spend.

That's us, at one end of a path, opposite the monks of Luang Prabang, who spend nothing: spending everything at one end, spending nothing at the other. Having to work for the rest of our lives at one end, never having to work at the other.

This is our trade-off.

The Save or Spend Trade Off

We could draw another chart. On the horizontal axis it could show what percentage of our income we spend every month. At one end, we have the perhaps impossible zen existence of no spending at all. At the other, a sadly much more typical existence of spending every single last penny until we have none left.

On the vertical axis it could then show how many years we have to work if we spend like that, from none if we spend nothing, to 100 (or infinity if we could draw that!) if we spend everything.

While these points where the line crosses an axis might be a bit too extreme to be useful in our daily lives, they're really useful from a theory standpoint: if you think about them, you know they're true.

If you spend 0% of your income, you never needed to earn that income. You don't need any of it, and if you keep living that way, you never will. At the other extreme, if you spend 100% of your income, you will have none left over to live on the next day, week, or month, and you will always have to earn more. And if you keep living that way, you always will.

Once we know these extreme points are true, we know there's a line between them where the points will be true too. We just have to calculate it.

So we did. Take a look at this chart.

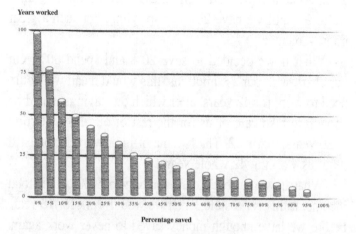

Years worked

Percentage saved

The intercepts are the same. Working for 100 years (standing in for infinity) or working for none.

Now we just have to draw a line between the two. The one we've drawn makes a few assumptions, the most important being that we manage to get a 7% investment return in a world with 3% inflation (a real return of 4%) – and once the combination of our savings and those returns reach 25× our spending, we never need to work again. How long that takes to happen, is shown up the vertical axis.

If we decide we shouldn't spend 100% of our income, and put 5% into our savings, we will no longer have to work an infinite number of years, but we will still have to work 78.

That's why the second bar on our chart drops to that level. Assuming we start work at 21, we'll be working until we're 99 until we have 25× our spending: not such a great improvement.

What if we decided to save 20% and spend 80%. On our chart, with our assumptions, this would mean we would need to work for 42 years, after which our savings would be enough to take care of us for the rest of our days. Starting at 20 years, that's 62. That's a major improvement, but still requires working 42 whole years!

What if we cut back our spending to 50% of our total income, if this is possible. Then we would work for 18 years before we have enough money saved to never work again. Starting at 20, that's 38 years of age.

If we could save 75% (I know how hard that sounds, but I also know people who do it), then we could be working for as short a period as 8 years.

Eight years. Start working in your 20s, be finished before your 30s.

Of course, if we could be truly zen, spending zero, we wouldn't need to work and we could just sit cross-legged all our lives.

Does this mean that everyone who works their whole life and never saves is wrong, while only people who work less than 10 years are right?

Of course not. We will never be happy with our lives if we make that kind of judgement.

We don't want judgement. We want knowledge. If you've never seen this chart or made this calculation before, you had no way of knowing how much life you were trading off for every few percentage points of your income you spend, but now you do. You now know.

Number Alert!

We've tried to keep numbers off most of the pages in this book. We think money is 98% psychology and 1% numeracy, and too many people spend all their time worrying about the 1% that doesn't add up!

If we get our heads in the right place, the numbers generally make sense of themselves.

But this is one occasion where we are going to have to think about the numbers, because what we are going to calculate is how much of our lives we work when we could have saved a bit more instead.

If that unsettles you, take a deep breath, then take a few more. Relax.

Be prepared to break the sums into simple parts to arrive at the final answer. We don't have to rush down our path. We can take it at our pace.

Let's start with a first example.

We can start by imagining we're saving 20% of our income every year. First, we should congratulate ourselves for doing a good job so far. By saving 20% of our income, we are following what is probably one of the best-known pieces of advice in personal finance: that half your budget should be spent on necessities, 30% spending on enjoyment and 20% to saving.

If we are saving 20%, we know from the chart above that we will need a 42-year working career, give or take, to build up assets worth 25× our spending.

If we start doing that at 20 years old, we will be a little over 60 when we're financially free. This isn't a bad outcome at all. It's better than most, so let's not judge ourselves unnecessarily.

But what if we do want to do better? Even if we're not ready to push ourselves much harder right now, we can still learn what difference it would make.

Take another deep breath – we're about to dive back into the numbers again!

Within our previous scenario, let's imagine that we're spending 10% of our annual income on expensive, once-in-a-lifetime holidays, every single year: that's one third of our enjoyment spending. It might seem extreme, but let's face it, not impossible.

If we didn't spend that money on those holidays, we could be saving 30% of our income, and shave 10 years off our career, cutting it by almost a quarter. Financially free in our 50s instead of our 60s.

That feels like a big deal, but also extreme, but what if we did half that, every two years? That would gain us five or six years of not working. Five or six years of freedom or two weeks of holiday every other year.

The point here is not to say "That's the right answer". It might be. It might not.

The point is to know, acknowledge, and fully understand the trade-off we are making.

If we know these numbers, and similar ones, we no longer live in ignorance. Previously, like Thoreau, you may have guessed you were swapping life for things, but you didn't know how many years of life you were actually trading. Now you do.

And you can breathe again!

How Much?

I don't think anyone has any idea of what they're spending money on. I think most of us have a pretty good idea of how much we're spending, because at the end of every month, we either have some money left in the bank or not. If we had some left last month, then that amount may have gone up or down a bit. Hopefully up.

But that's knowing roughly how much, not what we're spending it on, and not exactly how much on what.

There are a few ways we could do it. We could know what we spend a month and then divide that by 30. Or we could guess what we spend in an average day.

Or we could pull out a piece of paper and go back through the day, remembering hour by hour, thinking about all the occasions and places we have been when we could have spent, whether it was online, browsing for a book using an online reader, or out in the shops, stopping to fill the car, paying for a course, grabbing a bottle of water or snack. We could write how much we spent on each thing. We could look up receipts or credit card transactions.

If we wrote down the totals, and then did it every day, how close do you think it would be to our guess? Was it more or less? Or was it accurate?

If it was accurate, that may have been luck – most people are wrong. The 2009 Canadian study we mentioned in "The Saving Step" section found that people generally miscalculated their spending by at least 23%, and I have always assumed that a number between 25% and 30% would be about right.

My guess of 30% stems from "Miller's Law", which comes from a 1956 paper by George Miller of Harvard

University, "The Magical Number Seven, Plus or Minus Two", one of the most highly cited papers in psychology. As the title suggests, Miller's law argues that the number of things an average human can keep in their head, from a list of around 10, will be 7 (give or take 2).

So if we bought 10 things yesterday, we might remember 7 of them, forgetting 3. This is not small. If we are inaccurate by 30%, we may consistently be over-confident in our ability to save, or our ability to meet an unexpected cost – or even have 30% more unexpected costs than we anticipated!

That's 30% we might think we could have saved, and perhaps could have saved (if we had saved it first). That could be the difference between working our entire lives or retiring at 52. If you're not sure how important that is, ask a 53-year-old.

It also might be optimistic. More recent studies, such as one by Nelson Cowan at the University of Missouri, suggests that "working memory" is actually only good for saving four individual "chunks", not seven, and that the higher recall found by Miller was due to respondents remembering connected items together.

If our spending wasn't connected, we might not remember more than 4 of them. We might remember 4 out of 10 items, rather than forgetting 3.

We Need to Write Things Down

It has been theorised that the first form of writing was accountancy (which is really only the complicated word for writing down our spending!). The ancient Sumerians, living 5,000 years ago in an area that would now be Southern Iraq, were developing a culture and economy sufficiently complex that they could not keep it all in their heads, so they started to write it down.

"Bob owes Sheila 32 bushels of wheat" might have been impressed onto a clay tablet, or "the Seven Dollar Millionaire owes me seven dollars (again)" might be scratched onto another.

In some ways it is fascinating that such simple things needed to be written down, because human memories are capable of so much more. Concert pianists can learn unbelievably long pieces of music and actors remember every word in entire plays without ever writing them down. In our own worlds, we know we memorise an hour-long drive, turn by turn, without ever even trying to remember it. Once we get to a specific junction, we know what to do, which way to turn, even if we had forgotten this junction existed until we got to it.

Ancient story-tellers used this skill to tell their sagas, recounting whole books of exploits of mythic heroes, that were only to be written down much, much later, but there was no shopping list in their tales, nor expense budgeting. Everything was connected, and everything followed on, one from another, because that is how human memories work best.

Even the great memorists admit this, and use internalised storytelling-type techniques, such as the memory palace, to remind them of the items they need to remember on a list – which they would otherwise forget. As we all do, if we don't write it down.

We need to track our spending accurately. If we are going to become the masters of our spending (the alternative is to let our spending master us), then we need to know exactly what it is, and not let 30% slip by un-noticed (plus or minus 20%).

This is why we write it down.

Beyond Good And Evil

Remembering isn't the only reason we write it down. We want to contemplate our spending. We want to be able to look at the list of spending we made, and think about it, deciding whether we can learn anything from this spending.

This isn't about telling ourselves off for being bad spenders. It is just to be aware.

There may have been things on the list that we absolutely love, that gave us joy worth far more than the few pennies we paid. That's brilliant. Well done us!

There may also have been things we spent on that were less than amazing. Less well done us, but well done for noticing.

When we were developing *The Thousand Dollar Journal*, we organised a series of workshops with migrant workers in Singapore (if you don't know the background, Singapore is always at or near the top of the charts of the world's most expensive cities, and migrant workers are the lowest paid people there, and they're there to save money!).

One day, one participant said she was marking all of her spending as either "need" or "want". She didn't do it immediately, but she did it at the end of the week, when she was thinking about her spending for the week, and thinking if she could have cut back anywhere: if she could have spent a bit less and saved a bit more.

The other migrant workers in the group agreed it was a good thing, and asked if we could include a column in the "Spending Tracker" sheets in our Journals, so they could all do the same: so we did. If it worked for a migrant worker, the key users of the journal, then we weren't going to argue. The whole point of the journal wasn't for us to tell them what they were supposed to do, but help them do what they were already trying to do.

You can try the same if you like, although if your situation is less extreme than a migrant worker's life in the world's most expensive city, often living away from their families for years on end to make money for them, then you might not need such an extreme measure.

Separating between need and want can be useful, but it can also create problems, because it is highly subjective, not just between different people, but even for the same person on a different day: sometimes you really do need a bottle of water.

It could probably be labelled as a false dichotomy, where we group things into two groups, even though those two groups don't really exist. To visualise a false dichotomy, imagine a tape measure a metre long, with 50 centimetres as the middle marker. If we wanted to group the marks into two, it wouldn't be "wrong" to say that half of the marks are higher than 50 cm, and half of them are below.

It isn't wrong, but it doesn't tell us anything about the tape measure. It actually makes it sound like it is two collections of measures, where all the marks on one side have much more in common with each other than all the ones on the other. But 49 cm is on one side and 51 is on the other. And they're less than an inch apart.

That's a false dichotomy, and that can be what you're creating if you separate "need" and "want". They aren't necessarily "good" and "evil", but you've forced them into those categories.

You might be better off labelling them as something deliberately vague. "Yeah!" or "Meh". Or drawing a happy face and a frowny face next to them.

What you really want to ask yourself is this: was this spending worth more than the life I bought it with, and the life that it could have bought me in the future?

For some things, the answer is definitely yes. The rent I pay that stops me, my wife and children sleeping in the street is money well spent: I am glad I have that money to spend, and spend it willingly. The ice cream my daughter and I shared yesterday was brilliant. The ice cream wasn't earth-shattering, but the excuse to stop, sit down, take in our surroundings and enjoy them, was definitely worth more than a couple of dollars.

Once you have written it down, you can notice which spending made you happy (like ice cream), and which spending was avoiding real problems (like rent).

It won't always be the same answer. Sometimes you can buy an ice cream, eat it on your own, and feel a bit sick after. Sometimes you can over-spend on your rent.

Writing it down gives you the opportunity to notice where money is being well-spent, and where it is less well-spent, and give you the potential to redirect it.

This is what matters. Without noticing what we are doing, we can't know if we like what we are doing, if we think it is good for us or bad for us.

But we can't do this in our heads. I can't nor can you. We might be able to do it one event at a time, but not all of them, over a whole week, let alone a month. We have to write this down.

Seeing your reality directly is zen. If there is a point to meditation, it is to see ourselves and understand ourselves, and writing down our spending is doing that. Not writing it down is hiding from ourselves, and is not mindful.

Zen Spending Exercise

Write down your spending.

Write down today's spending so far. If that's not many items, write yesterday's. When that is done, write the day before.

When you are done, don't judge it. Just observe it. Think about whether it is accurate, but don't judge whether it is high or low.

Try it now. As much as closing your eyes and sitting in a cross-legged position, this is self-awareness. This is mindfulness and non-denial.

This is zen.

The Investing Step

Perhaps for more than any other part of our MISSION, the metaphor of a path is appropriate for investing – because it is now a confused path, criss-crossed by hundreds if not thousands of other tracks.

Some look like multi-lane highways that everyone says they are on, the guys on TV, the people on Twitter or Instagram, talking only about their good investments, never their bad ones.

Others look like muddy routes, too difficult for us to understand. Some look like fun, others look like hard work. Some have numbers, letters, combinations of them that make no sense: IRAs, ISAs, 401ks, ETFs, REITs, VTI, VIX.

Let's stop before we confuse ourselves. The point of the metaphor of the path is an important one. We know where we have come from, and we know where we are going. If we know why we are doing this, we will know which of the paths is straight ahead, pointing at our desired destination, and which ones we can avoid.

Let's not get distracted. Let's remind ourselves where we are going: we want our path to lead to financial peace of mind. If we don't have any "rainy day" savings, we need to clear our debt and get an emergency fund saved before we even think about investing. If we think about it too soon, it will confuse us more.

But once we have an emergency fund, once we know we could cover a difficult period, any extra money won't really help that purpose, and it could be earning more money, growing to become a much larger fund that could one day supplement or replace our entire income. That's our simple path.

"I Want What She's Having"

Let's imagine we are going for lunch together, you and me. We've selected a restaurant we haven't been to before but believe will be nice. Neither of us has any specific food requirements or allergies. We're both easy.

As we sit down at the table, we are presented with two menus. One, today's special set lunch menu offers a choice of three starters, three mains, and two desserts. The other is the size of a coffee table book, with page after page of courses, separated into meats, fish, pasta, mains, appetizers, sharing platters, and more.

I put the big book down, and immediately choose a starter and main course from the set. Three minutes later, you are still flipping from page to page and wondering if the fish is fresh.

More choice isn't always better. More choice is more ways to be wrong, and the confusion we feel about the potential for being wrong won't bring us happiness.

Quickly running some numbers might show us why we feel confused: 8 starters and 15 mains (ignoring dessert) makes 120 combinations. There's a less than 1% chance of ordering the chef's two best dishes. Add in just 5 desserts and there are 600 combinations. We could eat there for almost two years and not get the best three!

While you probably haven't done that precise equation, some part of your gut is communicating that low probability to you, and you're confusing it with hunger!

From the set lunch sheet, there's a one in three chance I will get the right starter, and a further one in three I will get their best main course. There's a more than 11% chance I will order perfectly.

One menu offers confusion, uncertainty, and less chance of winning. The set menu makes me confident, clearer, and happier. It is probably a little bit cheaper too, and the chef is likely to have put some of their better dishes on it, as they want us to come back. Win, win, win.

American psychology professor, Barry Schwartz, famously wrote about such examples in his 2004 book, *The Paradox of Choice – Why More Is Less*. We face choices in everything we do. In areas where we are expert, these choices can be wonderful, enabling us to choose from a multitude of different things, and get exactly the thing we want. In areas where we are not expert, the array is just confusing.

Back in the restaurant, someone near us has ordered something they clearly think is amazing. You put the menu down and say "I want what she's having!"

The Confused Path

With ordering out of the way, we sit down to discuss investing, the purpose of our lunch chat. We've had lunch chats in the past about money, income, our spending, and our saving, and we're now ready to discuss investing. Perfect.

I'm happy we're having the conversation because saving, while it has to come before investing (otherwise we'll have nothing to invest), won't get us as far down our path as we want to go. If you're heading for financial freedom, real financial peace of mind, you're going to need to invest.

Let's say you want to retire with a million dollars at the age of 70. If you only had saving as an option, and not investing, you would need to start saving $20,000 a year at the age of 20, and continue for 50 years until, coming to the end of your 69th year, the money in your savings account ticked up from $980,000 to a million. That's $1,666 a month, or $55 a day you need to save: it's not within reach for most of the planet. We probably shouldn't be eating lunch in such a smart restaurant.

Instead, if you can earn a 7% return on our investments, we need to save $7 a day, $210 a month, or $2,555 a year, and the 7% will compound our investments to be a million dollars in 50 years' time. The difference is staggering. Without investing, we would need to save 8 times more to get to the same amount.

But as we outlined before, there are so many ways to start getting these returns: people on the TV aren't us, the "finfluencers" aren't us, posh people representing expensive financial firms aren't us.

There are just so many paths to choose, more than we can imagine, and that translates into our mind not as opportunity but stress. We have so many ways to go wrong, so we stop and do nothing. It's easier to just spend the money today and worry about tomorrow tomorrow.

The Long-Term Power of Compounding

We write under the pseudonym of the Seven Dollar Millionaire for a number of reasons, but the biggest and best one is that it helps convey a simple idea: the huge long-term power of compounding.

Seven dollars, we calculated, is the smallest amount of money you need to save (and invest) every day to become a millionaire over the course of a typical 50-year career. That bit in brackets, the "and invest", is more important than you might at first think.

Because saving $7 a day will turn into roughly $2,500 a year, and then $125,000 over 50 years, if just saved and not invested. Investing it for just a 7% return (the S&P 500 has returned 9% on average for every 50-year period since the 1920s), will generate the other $875,000 required to turn it into a million dollars.

Doubling does amazing things to numbers. Two to four to eight, we all grasp. Eight to sixteen to thirty-two, is probably getting to most of our limits. But that is how much 7% returns compound over 50 years: $1 turns into $32. One year of saving $2,500 can become $80,000.

This is why we must take on the risk of investing. The risk of not investing is higher, because we will stand no chance of making those returns.

The Risk of Not Investing

Many people will tell you one reason they don't invest is because it is too risky. This is not true.

Investing well, which can also mean investing simply, can and should create a huge reduction in your total lifetime risk, while not investing at all can be, as the internet quotes everyone from Mark Zuckerberg to Warren Buffet as saying, the biggest risk of all.

Investing well means reducing our risks.

In fact, the reason there are so many inter-crossing paths at this point in our MISSION is because we all have different lives, we all have different needs, which means we all have different risks. Understanding our risks can help us understand which investments we should make, but because there are so many of us, with so many different types of risk, we don't know which one we should take, and this makes us incredibly uncertain. It is this uncertainty that stops people investing, not the risk.

Shortly, we will discuss an acronym I invented for my daughter called "R-RISK", which explains how we should treat risk when investing, but before we do that we need to understand that the biggest risk we can make when investing is not to invest at all.

Probably the most important concept we are not taught in school, in part because we aren't taught about money or investing, is that of "opportunity cost". What this term generally means is what our other best option is when we choose to do something. For example, if I choose to meditate this afternoon, I can't go for a walk at the same time; my opportunity cost is going for a walk. If I had been invited to play football, and I preferred that to walking, then my opportunity cost would have been playing football.

Because we can only do one thing with our time (most of the time) and one thing with our money, everything we do has an opportunity cost.

So if we consider investing to be risky, we can imagine what we do otherwise. Not invest: no risk there, surely. We can just keep our money, and it will still be money.

But we should consider that one day we will want to do something with that money. We could consider when that is likely to be, but also where that is likely to be, and what it is likely to be.

Are we going to want to buy a retirement apartment in Florida in 30 years? Are we going to want to pay for our kids' college in 10 years? Are we saving for a deposit on a property we hope to get in three years?

Between now and the time we want our money back, the global economy will have moved on. Things will have changed price. The food, the house, the apartment in Florida, the college fees: everything will have moved on. We know this because things have already been changing all our lives.

If you were born in the 60s, you will probably have watched a black-and-white TV at some point in your life, and thought colour was the greatest change imaginable. Born in the 70s, you will have experienced a childhood pre–music video, pre–computer games. Born in the 80s, computers will have sprouted everywhere in your childhood, while people born in the 90s will have seen computers go inside everything, from desktop to laptop to tablet to phone to watch. . . .

Some things get better and cheaper as the economy develops, while some things get more expensive – much more expensive – but nothing really stays the same. Not investing, keeping your money as money, will mean you take the risk that everything else stays the same value as your money today, even though you know that has never happened in the past. It is taking the most enormous risk which you know, deep down, is going to lose.

You have to embrace your uncertainty and take some better risks. R-RISK.

R-RISK

This five-letter acronym contains four ways of thinking about risk, and how we can reduce that without necessarily reducing our return. And that's the first two letters. . . .

Risk-Return: We combine these two words together, as there is strong evidence over history to suggest that they are very closely related. Things that have a higher risk of potentially losing money will need a higher return to compensate investors for taking that risk. Similarly, any opportunity with a low risk of losing money should have a lower return: if it doesn't, more investors will seek out that opportunity, and drive up the price (which will lower the return).

It feels a little self-defeating to mention this at the beginning of a section where we are talking about reducing risk, and also pointing out that taking no risk is the biggest risk of all, particularly as the main goal of this section is to encourage people to invest – but it is that important.

First, once you know that risks and returns are closely correlated, you can know not to trust people who tell you they aren't. If someone tells you they can make you a 20% return per year guaranteed, they are lying. The simplest way of spotting a scam is to know that the returns being promised don't match the risks being discussed. And avoiding scams is the most important thing we can do on our investing path.

Second, we can learn to take risks better, or take better risks, and by doing so increase our returns for the same amount of risk.

Integrity: That's what the I in R-RISK stands for. While this can mean honesty, which is good, we also take it to mean being true to ourselves: we should take risks we need to take, and avoid risks we don't.

Are you Filipino and plan on living there when you are older (if you currently live overseas or not)? If yes, you might want to invest in the Philippines stock market, and perhaps buy a house there.

Now go back to the paragraph above and change the name of the country to the USA, France, China, UK, Canada, Nigeria, Australia, Vietnam. Do it for each of those and see how it feels. And I mean "feels".

If one of those was the country you are from, and plan to live in, whether you are there now or you plan to return, the sentence with that word in may have generated a different reaction from the ones you are not from. Your spine may have tingled. Your stomach may have jumped or turned a little.

If none of those is your "home" country, then put that word in and see if it changes. Even if you don't get a physical or emotional reaction, roll the words around in your head. One will feel much more relevant to you than any of the others. Investing here will be an integrated risk, true to you, and not necessarily true to others.

You can have integrity in many other ways. You may want to avoid investing in things you feel are bad for people and the world, which can be done in increasingly positive and accurate ways, either by ESG (standing for environment, society, and governance) or impact investing.

You can have integrity by understanding when you are likely to want the money back that you are putting in, in 1 year, 5 years or 20 years, and make investments that either reward your longevity or don't punish you if you need it sooner.

It is why we can't repeat the famous line from *When Harry Met Sally* and "have what she's having". Because she's having what she needs, and that might not be right for us. She might be vegan. She might be lactose intolerant. She's her and you are you. You need and want different things.

Spread: The S is for spreading your risk around into different types of risk. Everyone's grandmother has told them "don't put all your eggs in one basket", but unfortunately, as none of us have carried eggs in baskets for decades, most of us have been uncertain how to use this truth.

I mean, some of us manage to work more than one job, so we aren't just reliant on that, and some people have more than one boyfriend and/or girlfriend as long as they can (until their energy runs out), but the term applies best to investing.

There is no reason to just have one type of investment, and in fact, it is dangerous to do that. Wherever possible we should diversify our risk, or spread it around.

In 1952, Harry Markowitz published a report in *The Journal of Finance* called "Portfolio Selection", that evolved into an entire subject called "Modern Portfolio Theory". Despite many arguments over its meaning and accuracy, this work won him the Nobel Prize in 1990 and became famous for its catchphrase: "diversification is the only free lunch in investing".

We aren't going to get into this theory in any detail, but what we need to understand is this: just as taking no risk is possibly taking the biggest risk, taking more risks, particularly different "uncorrelated" risks, reduces the level of risk for the return we get.

Remember how we said, just a couple of minutes ago in Risk-Return, that to get more return, we need to take more risk. Well, it turns out that if we take wider types of risk, more types of risk, and in particular risks that aren't correlated, meaning they don't go up and down together all the time, it can reduce our overall level of risk, not increase it. So we will, over time, make better returns with lower risks.

Knowledge: Taking more risks isn't something we should jump into blindly as soon as we start investing (although that doesn't mean we shouldn't start diversifying – it is still possible).

If we remember our earlier metaphor of the artist putting their first blob of paint on a blank canvas, our first investment can be like this. Not only is this our first exposure to the world of investing, it is our first opportunity to really learn about it. Over time, at our own pace, we can learn more and develop greater understanding of investing. This will be the other thing we can do to reduce our risk, and our feelings of uncertainty, by building our knowledge.

Building our knowledge steadily, surely, about the type of investing we need to do, that will get us to where we want to be, will be the thing that can most reduce our feeling of risk, or uncertainty, about our investments. This is how we can know we are on the correct path for us – and that's the K in R-RISK.

Once we acknowledge that nothing is risk-free ("zero-risk fallacy" is a cognitive bias just like confirmation or survivor bias), we can then appreciate we need to add risk to increase return, but we can do so carefully, selectively, in a diverse and integrated manner.

Small Regular Investments

Before we move on from investing, we need to consider another simplification we can make that can hugely increase our risk-return, and that is making small, regular investments rather than thinking we have to invest our life-savings in one go to feel like professionals.

There is a process called "dollar cost averaging", which means that you invest a regular sum of money every month. It could be dollars, but it could also be pounds or pesos – the point is that we invest the same amount every month, not buying the same number of shares every month, and by doing this we should get a better average entry price as shares move around.

Let's say we invest $200 a month in an index that in January costs $10 a share. We buy 20 of them. In February, the price has come down to $8, so our $200 buys us 25 shares. In March, the price has gone up to $12.50, so we buy 16.

If we had spent $600 in January, we would have bought 60 shares with our $600, but if you go back and add them up, we have 61 shares.

We have got a magic little share for free because we bought more when they were cheap, and less when they were expensive. Looked at another way, if we had thought to ourselves, "I want to buy 20 shares a month", it would have cost us $610 to buy them during those three months.

Making small regular investments works. It works for people saving regular amounts of money, transferring their savings automatically to investments at the beginning of every month, and it works because they end up with cheaper investments.

I do this myself. Just this month, I have started investing in a new asset class that I had stayed out of because I didn't know enough. After doing a little bit of homework, I realised I needed some exposure, but I didn't like the risk of moving all my money at one go, so instead I am buying a bit more, every few weeks, the same amount of money every time, hoping to get a better average entry cost.

Zen Investing Exercise

Please think about what integrity means to you. Think about what your path could look like, what you would like it to contain. Think about what could bring you peace of mind and security.

Write it down if that helps but spend time just thinking about it deeply. What do you want your world to look like, and how do you want your money and assets to fit within that?

If you haven't already, start researching index funds or exchange-traded funds that might fit best to your integrity, whether that's a global equity fund, the S&P 500, or an ESG or impact fund.

And then make a plan to start buying a regular amount of that at regular intervals. Set a start date for doing this, as soon as possible: this could change your life.

The Owning Step

"When you realise nothing is lacking, the whole world belongs to you."

—*Lao Tzu*

Owning means three things to me. It means owning assets, things that will pay back over time more than they cost.

This is the end goal of investing. It is the biggest difference between speculating – guessing if one thing is going to go up in price faster than another – and investing, where we feel a sense of ownership of an asset, whether it's a house, a business, or a 0.000001% stake in a company. We own it.

Ownership also means not having debt to own those assets: debt means other people own them, not us.

But perhaps more than those two, owning means owning the process, taking full responsibility for what's happening.

No one else will care enough about your financial peace of mind to ensure you achieve it. You need to do that. Only you can care enough to know what your journey should entail, and make that journey. No one else can and no one else will care enough to walk the walk for you. The path is yours.

If you are going to achieve proper financial peace of mind, and even financial freedom, you are going to have to do this your own way, and own this.

Freedom from Financial Concerns

Let's remember one of the places our path could potentially lead: financial freedom. While this can sound like such an avaricious phrase, the word "finance" coming first, it is really the precise opposite.

It is the freedom from financial concerns. It is stopping worrying about money.

Financial freedom will not bring about freedom from family concerns, health concerns, locational concerns. It can reduce work concerns only if we work for money, and that is what our concerns are about. If we work for personal achievement, to create great art or to satisfy bigger goals, financial freedom won't bring us freedom from those concerns.

As the famous one-liner so perfectly puts it: "Money is better than poverty, if only for financial reasons."

But financial reasons are not small reasons. Even with the simplest lifestyle, we need a roof over our head, we need a table in the kitchen to put food on, and then we need to put food on that table. These basic things alone can occupy a huge amount of our days.

What if we owned the house? That would remove the need to work to pay the rent. If that costs one third of our income, as many budgeting recommendations suggest it should, that is one third of our life we no longer need to work to pay the rent. We could work less, or work differently, or save more, or just worry less about our finances.

What if we owned assets that paid income to cover the food on the table? If that's another 20% of our incomes, we would have another big chunk of our lives freed up from working for money. We could still work for other things, but that reason would be gone.

That's financial freedom. And that's how ownership attains that.

Debt Is Not the End

We have not discussed debt much so far. This is because debt adds to financial worries, it doesn't answer them. In the same way money is a store of energy and time, debt is the opposite, and it will grow constantly. We will need to pay more back, and the amount will keep on increasing.

Any debt we have reduces our assets and therefore reduces our ownership. This doesn't mean we must never borrow: it just means we should only ever borrow to buy things that will enable us to pay back our debt more easily than otherwise.

Consumer debt won't do that. Credit card debt can't do that. What it can do is double in just two to three years. These expensive forms of debt will come at the cost of our future livelihoods. Borrowing to buy a car might be worthwhile if it is the cheapest car you can afford, the cheapest debt you can afford, and having a car helps you earn money.

Perhaps the greyest area for borrowing is student loans for college and university. With increasing amounts of education now freely available online, and prices for the offline version increasing faster than almost any form of inflation, it's not surprising that Professor Scott Galloway of NYU Stern calls elite colleges "a fetish – believing you are a luxury brand instead of a public servant."

If you really can't find an alternative to borrowing for that, here's your report card: "try harder."

The reality is that your chosen degree will need to ensure that your subsequent career pays enough that you can save and pay back around 20% of your total tuition fees every year, or the impact of interest costs will mean the value of the loan starts to grow faster than your earnings, and you will just be servicing the interest. You may have been better off with no degree and no debt.

Even borrowing to buy a house isn't necessarily a no-brainer. Because the bank owns the house until you have paid the debt, and houses generally go up in price, banks offer very low interest rates on mortgages. That's the good thing.

Unfortunately, because houses are so expensive, banks will often lend 90% of the price of the house, or even more, to people putting down just a 10% deposit. That's wonderful if the house goes up in price: a 10% increase equals a 100% gain for the buyer. But if the house goes down in price by 10%, and the buyer can't cover their mortgage, they can lose their whole deposit. That might be their life's savings.

It's why a house with a mortgage shouldn't be your only asset, and why you shouldn't be saving up for your dream home, because it could turn into a nightmare, and you won't actually own it until you've paid off all of that debt.

But done sensibly, borrowing against a property can help you build an asset base that can move you towards future financial freedom.

Financially Free

What we really want to own is our lives: the course of our lives, what we do with them, who we help, what we achieve, how we feel about them. The more time we spend earning money or worrying about where the next dollar will come from, the less free we are, the less we own our lives.

The formula for financial freedom is that we need 25 times our annual spending. This is because we should be able to invest our assets to get a return of 7% or better (the S&P 500 has returned 9% in every 50 year period over the last 90 years), which will allow us to take out 4% every year, leaving in 3% or more to cover the cost of inflation.

How did I find this out? I spent quite some time calculating it myself, but then at almost exactly the same time stumbled across Mr Money Mustache and the Rockefeller Foundation. One is a leading financial endowment that has been paying out 4% of its assets for more than 100 years; the other is a leading light of the FIRE movement. Poles apart, but they both use the same equation.

How does this work?

1. Let's say you need $10,000 a year to live.

2. If you have $250,000 in assets, earning 7%, that's $17,500.

3. If you take out $10,000 for the year, you'll have $257,500 left, 3% more than you had last year.

4. A 7% return on that new higher number is $18,025 and you can take out $10,300 (up 3% to cover inflation)

5. Leaving in $7,725 will mean you now have $265,475.

6. And so on.

You take out 4%, you leave in everything you make above 4%, and the assets you have should last forever. It's that simple. But obviously that isn't easy. A lot of people will look at those numbers and think:

- $10,000 isn't enough for me to live on.

- And I can't save $250,000.

It is one of those things that seems almost ridiculously impossible before we start, it is so far away, but patient and steady steps will get us there. Owning the process, saving first, controlling what we spend, will steadily move us towards it.

A FIRE of Your Own

(A version of this section was first published in the wonderful UK magazine, *The Idler*, dedicated to "fun, freedom and fulfilment", in their financial column, "Easy Money", written by our British cousin, the Seven Pound Millionaire.)

When Vicki Robins and partner Joe Dominguez, authors of the 1992 financial independence classic *Your Money or Your Life*, hit the road in their van in the 1980s, they blazed their own trail espousing the virtues of FIRE (financial independence, retire early). While an increasing number of FIRE enthusiasts have since followed suit, they don't all follow the same route and the road branches off in what can seem surprising directions.

Despite your scepticism, thinking that owning assets worth 25× annual spending is too far off, one of these alternative paths might be the right one for you.

The term Fat FIRE has been christened for the few people who do find it easy to save 25× their annual spending, and so their plan is to accumulate enough assets such that 4% a year affords a lavish lifestyle. Travelling in business class perhaps or sipping champagne on a yacht in the Mediterranean. This is extreme, but the 4% rule still holds. Fat FIRE is 25× an expensive life, and if it were the only route, it would be a long and probably impossible path for most of us.

Lean FIRE is its obvious opposite, focusing on cutting living costs to an absolute minimum. This has two benefits. First, the total you need to save to get to 4% or 25× is much lower. Spend $40k a year, and you need $1,000,000 total assets (25 × 40k). Spend $20k a year, and you only need half a million in your nest egg. Second, by cutting back on your expenditure today, you'll be saving at a much faster rate (using this last example, an extra $20k a year), and moving towards this goal faster.

Lean FIRE enthusiasts tend to be the most evangelical in their frugality and investing, but what they achieve can be truly inspiring. Save 75% of your annual income and you can be financially independent in just 8 years. Start work at 22 and "retire" by 30. That sounds unlikely, but it is not only mathematically possible, people have done this, and are doing it all the time, without working highly paid jobs.

You don't necessarily have to live in a campervan, but my social media bingeing has shown me enough Lean FIRE fans in four-wheel homes for me to rename them "Van FIRE" in my head. Of course, the campervan makes perfect sense as an extremely low-cost way to live while achieving FIRE, and then travel once it's achieved.

Travel is something we all look forward to having more time to do in retirement, whether early or not, but it also plays an additional role in some versions of FIRE, often referred to annoyingly as "geo-arb", but which might sound nicer as Wander FIRE.

This has actually been with us for a long time. Probably as many Brits have a grey-haired relative in Chianti-shire or the Dordogne, who picked up their villa for a song, and now souse themselves slowly in summer sun and local wine, as Americans have family retired to Florida. In the FIRE community, this geo-arb tends to be more extreme, of course, with proponents living on tropical beaches in Costa Rica for peanuts a month, lowering the total amount they need to make the sums work.

Eco FIRE, or socially conscious FIRE, is another spin-off that merges the trends of environmentalism and fair-trade with financial independence. It might seem incongruous that a movement that starts with financials, literally, could be so left-leaning, but it feels less jarring when considering that FIRE usually has mindful consumption at its core, encourages independence and less need for "the system".

There is also a very strong correlation between spending less money and saving the environment, after all. It obviously isn't the savings of the top 1% that causes 50% of global

CO_2 emissions, according to Oxfam; it's their spending. Getting them to save money, getting all of us to save money, will help.

Coast FIRE is a little closer to the mainstream. This branch of the movement acknowledges all the key tenets of FIRE such as the 4% withdrawal, frugality, and investing, but also the existence of real life, like children, the mortgage you took on before discovering FIRE, a spouse that might not be as keen as you on living in a van, and that saving and investing steadily towards the target might be more sensible. Rather than saving 75% of your income for 8 years, more like 30% for 40 years, perhaps, but achieving the same end. "Financially independent retire eventually", might be a more appropriate acronym for Coast FIRE, and not such a bad idea.

Coast FIRE also covers groups who have funds already invested that will become their 25× nest egg in the future, as long as they don't touch it just yet. They continue working in a job they enjoy for now, and perhaps forever, covering their basic living costs while enabling their investment fund to grow untouched. The importance of health insurance to Americans has created an additional path known as Barista FIRE, wherein a part-time job at Starbucks covers their insurance, their salary covers basic costs, and their investments compound unimpeded.

One of these paths, Coast or Eco, Fat or Lean, may work for you. They may not, and you may need to beat your own path to financial freedom. That is fine. That is how you own this.

You could take inspiration from zen practice, and believe you could perform zen FIRE, needing as close to nothing as it is possible to need, not even a van or the Instagram account that #vanlife necessitates.

Instead, you may decide that some things are really important to you, and will always be really important to you, and you work to own that asset, or the assets that will pay for you to enjoy those things for the rest of your life.

You could take issue with the importance of the word "retirement" in the acronym FIRE, as many financial enthusiasts do, and perhaps focus on creating FI-Zen, a path to financial independence that enables you to feel zen about everything.

Do it your way. That is how you own this.

Zen Owning Exercise

If you have been tracking what you spend monthly, you can now calculate what 300× that would be. That's the same as 25 times your current annual spending and would mean you can take out 4% and live on it forever.

If that total seems unreasonably high, then you can calculate a smaller number, a basic living expense, and then 300× that. This total could give you more financial peace of mind.

Whichever number feels more realistic, plan what assets you would like these totals to be in: how much in property (if you live in it, it will cover your rent but not contribute to your other spending), how much in equities, indexes, bonds or other assets? How much can you invest into tax-free plans?

This won't be accurate, it can't be, but it can start drawing the picture of what you are aiming for.

The Now Step

"The best time to plant a tree was 20 years ago. The second-best time is now."

—*Orchard owners (and the internet)*

Investments, like trees, require time to grow. A tree that was a seedling 20 years ago is something you can climb in today. It might bear fruit, it might also give shelter. It did it on its own: you just planted it.

Without the time machine required to plant a tree 20 years ago, the best thing you can do is plant a tree today, and then you will enjoy it 20 years from now. If you don't, in 20 years' time, you'll wish you had.

As the internet would say: "This isn't about planting trees."

The Boring Power of Compounding

The following phrases are also popular on the internet: "Compounding is the eighth wonder of the world," and "compounding is the most powerful force in the universe." Bizarrely, these quotes are regularly ascribed to Albert Einstein, to give them more mathematic kudos along with popularity, although there is no evidence he ever said either of them, and it is unlikely he would have done.

He also didn't say: "Compounding looks really boring to start with, so we ignore it, but it becomes so massive over time that most of us don't know how to calculate it." I know that quote is much less popular, and wasn't Einstein's, because I wrote it just now, googled it to check, and I am pretty certain no one has ever said it before, let alone Einstein. But it's true.

We discussed how important compounding is when looking at why we need to invest, but it is so important a topic to understand, that we're also going to talk about it now, while thinking about why it is important to invest "now".

To start with, compounding looks pathetic. Sorry, but you need to be ready for that. The first few years of investing and getting reliable returns can feel like being a kid in biology class, waiting for a seed to sprout.

"Come on! Hurry up! Nothing is happening! I think mine is broken!"

But compounding, which means growth on top of growth, soon gets faster. Much faster. That seed will turn into a tree.

Let's use an example: a 10% return means you get $10 on a $100 investment in a year. Our linear brains can then imagine it takes 10 years for that investment to become $200, and then another 10 for it to become $300, so 30 to become $400, 40 to become $500 and 50 to become $600. $10 a year, $100 every 10 years. Simple.

We might sense that's a little bit wrong, but not quite how wrong. A 10% return actually doubles in roughly seven years, not 10, because every year, the amount the investment grows is now growing on top of the new total. Year two's return isn't $10, it's $11, because it's 10% of $110.

So far, I can assume you agree with the first half of my unquotable quote, that compounding is really boring to start with.

"Big deal," I assume you are thinking, because I remember thinking it myself, we were wrong by a dollar. But the dollars add up, and instead of doubling in 10 years, it doubles in seven, and then continues to double every seven, so that instead of $100 making $500 in 50 years, $100 makes $12,700. Yes, $12,700!

There is only one tiny difference between the two calculations that generate such different answers. In the first example, we earn $10 every year on $100, and we take that $10 away and spend it. Doing it this way, we really would get earnings of $500 off that $100 in 50 years.

In the second example, we leave the $10 there, so next year grows on that $10, and, while we're not watching, it grows into a tree. That's the whole point of compounding: we leave the growth there for it to grow on itself next year.

Here's the thing. You have to start now. You can't short-circuit the first few boring years: they have to happen. If the boring years don't happen now, they happen later.

The formula for becoming a Seven Dollar Millionaire involves saving $25,000 in the first ten years, between the ages of 20 and 30, and investing it so it becomes $35,000. In the next 10 years that doubles to $70,000, then to $140,000, then to $280,000. In the last 10 years of our working career, that doubles again to $560,000. We saved $25,000 but it became $560,000 from investing.

But if we wait 10 years before making that saving, it will only become $280,000. Waiting 10 years before starting to save that $25,000 costs us $280,000!

Live in the Present

Be present. Be in the moment. There is only now.

It can seem odd discussing thinking about the future, planning and saving for the future, while also talking about zen, with its focus on being present. It can feel very un-zen to plan for the future.

It is not.

We shouldn't fantasise or over-worry about the future. It may be neither as good or as bad as we fear. It is bad to live in the current moment thinking about the next, wondering if it will be better, or worse. That is definitely un-zen.

But the future is coming. You will be older. You will have different needs. This is reality, and zen is to see the world, our nature, as it is. Not hide from it. Not fantasise about it. This is simple. This is zen.

The money you do not need today you may need in the future. If it can compound for you, you can do more with it then. This is reality.

Now

More than anything, now is the only time where change can take place. Anything deferred is something that gets deferred again and again and again.

Part of chronic procrastination is the belief that something will be different in the future that will enable us to do a thing that we aren't doing today. Stephen Pressfield in *The War of Art* calls this resistance, and anything that stops us doing what we know we should do needs to be fought.

A zen frame of mind will tell you that the only time it can change is now. A book won't get written in retirement if you can't write it before. A holiday won't enable you to meditate if you can't look away from your phone today.

A seed planted today will turn into a tree. One that isn't planted will always remain a seed.

There is only now.

Zen Exercise

For every other step in our MISSION, we have had a zen exercise. For this one, we have 49.

Start now.

Chapter Three
The Path Is Practice

―∽―

First Steps

The way we normally talk about walking is to say that one step comes after another, which of course it does.

But one step has to come first. Without that first one, the second can't happen, nor can any of the others.

The first thing to do is to take the first step, but what if you're not sure which step you should take?

In the following pages we suggest 49 steps. You could do one a day, seven a week, for the next seven weeks. You can do a few in a row, bunching a chunk of activity into one day. Some of them might become daily habits that give you control over your money, and peace of mind. Some could lead to an emergency fund or nest egg. Some are just nice and cheap, often free, and will get you started on your path.

We suggest you try them all, one after another. You can jump around if you like, but start with this first one, and as we said at the end of Chapter Two, start now.

Step 1: Saving Comes First

As saving always comes first, the first step must be to open a new account and put money into it.

This could be a savings account at your bank, a robo-advisor app on your phone or an investment account at a broker, online or offline. If you don't have any of those, start with the first.

Once you have one of those – or if you already have all of them – put some money in that account.

Please try to do it now.

While you're at it, calculate a small sum that you can afford to have regularly transferred into that account, and arrange for that.

When we meditate, it is common to set an intention at the beginning. With finance, intention setting is important, but practice is everything.

As you're reading this, we think you already have the intention to save so create somewhere to put that saving, and put something in it right now.

This could take as little as 10 or 15 minutes. If this is the account that kick-starts your saving habit and results in your financial security or even freedom, it could be the most valuable 15 minutes of your life. Please do it now.

Step 2: Count to 10

Put down whatever you're holding and count to 10, one count for each in-breath. Do it now.

I did it. I took a medium breath, not super-big like you would do to show off or dive under-water, but big enough to notice, and counted "one".

The goal is to think about your breathing for 10 breaths. You'll think about other things, of course you will, but by remembering to count, it can bring your focus back to your breathing.

I immediately thought about what I was going to write next, this bit, about how breathing is the one body activity between our conscious and subconscious, that we do totally without thinking (like our heart-beat or digestion), but can almost totally control too, unlike our heart-beat or digestion. For some reason, I then thought about how in movies there are sometimes super-heroes who can stop their heart beating, and then I remembered I had skipped a breath and needed to count "three".

If your attention or focus is like a muscle, this exercise is like a bicep curl, flexing it, bringing it back. But it's better than that. The fact that you're breathing deeper, exhaling more CO_2 from your lungs can help reduce your blood acidity, reducing anxiety and even pain. Where was I? "Five".

If it's the same for you, thoughts interrupting all the time, that's fine.

It might be the same for zen monks. They look calm on the outside, but who knows what they're imagining inside? They could be fighting Shao-lin style against a magical serpent dragon I see in my head as being drawn in black and white Japanese anime-style. And I'm not even at "eight" yet.

It's ok. Any number is the right number to just think about breathing again. I can think about my stomach going out as my diaphragm pulls down to make space in my chest, air rushing in through my nose, before being pushed out again. That's "nine".

But even if those zen masters do really feel as though they're floating on clouds, not fighting every stupid thought they get like I have been, it's because they've been practicing so long and hard, and maybe they started like this. Maybe their first session of breath-focused meditation began with 10. With just 10 breaths.

Please give it a try now.

Learning to breathe properly can be life-changing. A minute of good breaths can improve the next 10 minutes, and that can improve the next hour, and that can improve the whole day. Done every day, that could improve your life, but even if it doesn't, it's free and takes a minute. That's a great risk-return scenario.

Don't do anything else immediately after. Maybe another 10 breaths, or just see if you feel a little different, perhaps a little calmer. If you do, just enjoy that sensation for as long as it lasts.

Step 3: Write Down Your Spending

Stop what you're doing and get a pen and piece of paper. Don't read on until you have it ready.

With pen poised and the blank sheet in front of you, write down everything you spent money on today or yesterday. Don't judge what you spent on, judge your recall. The game is to make sure you remember everything, not to imagine a small total.

I'll share mine, although it's a bit rubbish: my back hurt, so I stayed in all day, and didn't spend anything. Thinking a bit harder, though, I remember I got a text message last thing in the evening from my daughter that she needed a deposit immediately for her new flat (she's starting a new year at college), and so I sent money to her account. So there was something, and it was quite a lot!

What does yours look like? I hope, even if it was more complicated than that, it was still a lot cheaper. If it was too easy, perhaps go back another day.

The day before had more going on. Thinking back, I met a friend for coffee, but he paid. What about lunch? I packed lunch from home, a left-over salad from the day before.

Damn, I've got nothing. But I drove to work, and parked my car, and although the money for that is stored on a pre-paid card, so there was no "cash out" that day, it was still spent then, so I can record it.

Did I buy nothing else? Anything on the internet? I bought some new running shorts in an online sale that I won't be using for a while now with my bad back, but I think I bought those the day before yesterday, or even earlier, not yesterday.

You can see how tricky the exercise can get – that's why it's so important to do it as soon as possible. Writing down everything either in the evening of the same day or the morning after is the best way to know exactly what you're doing.

This could become a simple part of a journaling exercise: noting down what you did the day before. While writing down what you did, how much it cost, you could also note how it made you feel, if it was worth it, if other things were better, how you feel about it today.

Knowing what you're doing is a basic form of self-awareness. Nothing is more zen.

Step 4: Breathe More

Do you feel like focusing on your breathing for a little longer than 10 breaths?

If yes, set a timer on your watch or phone for 5 minutes, sit somewhere comfortable, or even lie down, and close your eyes. You can choose to count your breaths if you like, or instead just focus on the sensation of breathing.

There's lots of it, after all. Sensation, I mean.

It's one of the least appreciated factors of life that there is too much information to take in. This isn't just the modern-world phenomenon of information overload, but it has always been the case. Even with your eyes closed, you can still feel across your whole body, hear any sound that is being made within earshot and smell any trace elements with aroma in the air around you. Your brain can process many of these in the background, but in the foreground has to focus on one, or at most just a few, shoving everything else into the background.

It's natural for our minds to rotate between all of the different inputs, appreciating one, then another, then another. But that natural cycling between one stimulus and the next can also result in our restlessness, a lack of focus or concentration, and also frustration. Learning how to notice that happening, and maybe slow it a little (and maybe not) is one of the joys of being a bit more mindful and can roll over into other enjoyment.

So close your eyes and breathe.

Afterwards, do something chilled out that lets you enjoy the perhaps more calm frame of mind you now have. Enjoy.

Step 5: Collect Receipts

It may be hard to do this right now, as it is unlikely you're buying anything and being issued a receipt at the exact moment you're reading this, but you can do three things right now instead that will make it easier.

First, set the intention to collect a receipt for every purchase. Easy.

Second, decide on a system for collecting the receipts. You can collect physical receipts, gather them in your wallet, purse or pocket, and then empty them at a regular interval into a bowl, envelope, box or folder. Or you can collect digital receipts of online shopping, photographing physical ones on your phone. Or you can find an app that does all this for you. They exist.

Three, then decide how often you'll look at them, and when. Daily? Weekly, on a Saturday morning, to see how the week before has gone, and to decide if you need to be careful this weekend? Or should you do it monthly, reluctantly, before giving up?

Four, guess which one of the options is least likely to work. I am kidding. It's the last one. Try one of the others, and keep track of what you're doing.

Step 6: Build The Faith

Some forms of meditation involve reciting a mantra. Some forms will suggest a mantra in a language that means nothing to you, and some will charge you good money for that mantra.

We're not going to do that.

We're going to find our own mantra, that means something useful to us, and work out how and when we're going to say it. We aren't going to worry about how this works, or even if it works at all. Sports people take practice shots without any equipment to prepare their mind for what they're about to do, without knowing if or why it works. You are about to change your mind about money – you should do the same.

Think about who you are, what generally motivates you, what dreams you may have, and how you can capture the essence of that in a short phrase.

"I am going to fix my finances for my family" could be the phrase you need to hear from yourself. If it is, start saying it to yourself now, regularly.

"I can make me a millionaire" might be your mantra.

"I am developing new habits that will help change my life" might be what you need to shoot for.

If none of those is quite right – they probably aren't – take the time now to play around with different words to see how they repeat in your head. They should be ambitious enough to make you slightly embarrassed, so they capture your emotional response and you feel it in your gut, and not just your head, but not so unrealistic that you can't even say them to yourself. You could start by doing those 10 breaths from Step 2. Carry on counting on the in-breath, one, two, etc., but on the out-breath, think your one thought. Build your faith in yourself.

If you are starting to journal by recording your expenses, you could finish each day's practice by writing down your mantra, perhaps evolving it over time.

Step 7: Look Back, Look Ahead

If you have been doing one of these a day, you've got a week under your belt.

If you have taken all seven steps, one day at a time, you're amazing. I am so impressed, I want you to write to me, and let me know. Please, I really want to hear all about it. You can find contact details on our website www .sevendollarmillionaire.com.

If you haven't done them all, it's not a big deal. There's no judgement necessary. If you've done some but not all, maybe check back and see the ones you can try out today, catching up a bunch in one block. Some of them only take a minute.

Have a think about the ones you liked and the ones you didn't. I don't mind if you don't like them all. Not everything is right for everyone. I am just trying to give suggestions. It's good for you to be honest with yourself, and ask why you didn't like them though, and whether it's because they're difficult for you.

If you didn't do any of them though, can I please ask you to stop reading now, and do one? If you keep reading to the end of the book, without stopping, you are likely to put it down and forget about it. If you do one thing now, it could build the habit of doing more, and this will help you change. Pick any one you like from the last six – and do one now before you look at the next word.

Once you've looked back, try looking ahead. Think about which of these you can take into the next week or beyond. Taking 10 breaths, reciting a mantra, and keeping track of your spending should be fast and easy to do going forward. Putting some money into your savings account could change your life. Set the intention to do at least some of them again, in addition to the new practices this week.

Baby Steps

We can sometimes lose momentum after the first couple of steps.

It can be tempting to jump too far ahead, believing we are now experts in this new area, taking on challenges that become too uncomfortable and make us want to quit.

Or we can experience the opposite, experiencing disquiet with the changes already made, and wondering if they are for us.

Now is the time for small footsteps on the path: ones we know we can make easily, ones that may just be a little bit of fun. This doesn't need to feel hard or boring to work: in fact, the opposite.

Take fun little steps and the path will be easier.

Step 8: Make a Zen Tracker

I had the wonderful good fortune to chat to John Paul Flintoff, author of *How to Change the World* and *A Modest Book About How to Make an Adequate Speech* (could there be a better combination of book titles?), on a Zoom call. To my surprise, he generously took the time to show me how to fold a piece of A4 paper into an eight-page booklet, or "signature", that will fit inside the smallest of pockets.

It was a privilege bordering on embarrassment to have a best-selling author show me how to fold paper, but in many ways, it was like being taught to sit still by a zen master. John Paul uses this booklet in all manner of wonderful ways, to note, sketch, and jot down thoughts. He then even stitches them together, using a needle and thread, to see what flicking through a book like that might feel like.

He knows much, much more about putting a book together than I do, but the process of always having a booklet handy to jot down something can be valuable for all of us. For example, we can use them for tracking our week. We could track our spending, our saving, our great ideas, our meditation thoughts or our mantras to remember or as they occur to us.

I can't tell you how to fold the paper like he did, because I struggle to remember myself, but it really only involves three folds and one small cut. If you look on Youtube, you will find some videos that show you how to do it in less than a minute, and there will be your notebook.

What's even better, it will be one you made, so it will mean more to you and it should have cost nothing. More value and money saved!

Once you have your booklet, you can label it "My Zen Tracker" or anything you fancy. Perhaps "An Even Littler Book of Zen Money". You could give it a front cover, and then label the seven days of the week after it, or start on the front with a weekday, and save the back cover for a gathering together of the week.

My favourite thing to do is draw an ensō, on the front, symbolising both simplicity and infinity – although I should confess I don't draw them nearly as well as Soo, who made the ones illustrating this book.

Making the drawing is an act of meditation and intention itself, and it reminds me of that whenever I look at it. It also looks like a zero, which reminds me how much I should be spending!

Step 9: Important . . . Notice

This one is perhaps the simplest exercise so far, but also the hardest – and maybe the most valuable. Let's try to notice things more today.

Our attention is valuable, so valuable the biggest companies in the world essentially treat our attention, and their ability to attract it and keep it, as their primary asset. But it should be even more valuable to us. We talked about our lives consisting of time and energy in The Path Is A MISSION, which is true, but our lives are also what we notice, what we care to think about or remember. Noticing is living.

We may think we do this, and we hopefully do, but we can do it more, and this can feel like living more. Perhaps because we're rested, perhaps because we're seeing more new things, we tend to notice more on holiday: foreign sunsets may seem more beautiful, but it is the same sun setting over the horizon wherever you are. We can't always be on holiday, but we can bring that noticing mind with us instead.

You can try this in two ways today. You can, if you have time, really spend some time noticing something familiar, perhaps something on the table or desk in front of you. Anything. If you're in a coffee shop, has someone spilt some sugar that hasn't been cleaned up, and is the sun refracting through the crystals? Or isn't it? Are they just pale white specks? Right now, there will be something you haven't noticed. Give it some extra time, and you are giving yourself extra time. Make it a practice, and you will find this leads to a greater appreciation of your circumstances.

You won't always see that holiday sunset, but you will see it more often if you look for it.

The second way is to "double-take". Take an extra split second to register something's existence. This could be saying its name in your head. "Stapler" is the first thing I could double-take, as it is right in front of me, but if you had asked me just 10 minutes ago if I had a stapler on my desk, I wouldn't have known the answer. This simple practice can help develop more awareness, and boost your attention.

Together, these two practices can help us develop more focus and presence, less distraction. If you have already made your "zen tracker", you could write down some of the things you notice there.

Step 10: Secret Zen Tracker

Have you made the little notebook from Step 8 yet? Please give it a go. They are surprisingly joyful little things.

At the most prosaic, they're great places to keep note of your spending. You can slip a few receipts into the pages before you note them down on their specific day, or whatever you like to use them for. They're great for removing the excuse of not being able to record what we're doing, which can help us build our awareness.

But they have an extra little secret. Like an antique desk, these notebooks have a hidden compartment. Unfold the booklet to A4 size again, and you'll see you've only been writing on one side of the paper. If you reverse the folding process, you can fold the book back up again, but this time with only the blank side showing. A whole new notebook for you to use in secret.

What do you want to keep secret? Maybe you don't want to share your meditations or mantras with people. Maybe you don't want anyone to see the spending you have been tracking. Or maybe you'd like to keep track of both, and just flip the book around to whichever one you want to use then.

You have two notebooks for the price of one, and the first one was free!

Step 11: Better Get a Bucket

In a world with so much information to process, even for something as powerful as the human brain, we create short-cuts to interpret and understand that information.

When we hear about "cognitive biases", it is normally in a negative context, reflecting a supposed error in our thinking. Thought processes such as confirmation bias, where we only accept new information that confirms our view, can have negative outcomes for us, particularly as they are often unconscious and we don't realise we are thinking this way. Perhaps the most negative cognitive bias is just that, "negativity bias", where we greet all information as bad, or remember only the worst things that happen, which can lead to pessimism or even depression.

But we can use cognitive biases in our favour, as that is what they are designed to do, and the best way to do this is to use them consciously. We have hinted at that when discussing framing, and even mantras, but finance has its own cognitive bias we can use for our benefit, which is technically called mental accounting bias, but I prefer to call it "the bucket bias".

Mental accounting bias reflects that we, as humans, aren't particularly good at thinking about money, because it is just numbers, and instead we are better when we think about things, even if they're abstract things like holidays and pensions.

So most people tend to save a bit better when they separate their saving into separate buckets: "$100 for my pension, $200 for a deposit for a house, and $50 towards a holiday later this year" for example. Another example could be when building an investment portfolio: "$1,000 into an index fund, $800 into stocks, $200 into crypto".

By thinking of our savings goals targeting specific things, or just breaking it into chunks, we are better able to handle the individual concepts. This can make us more comfortable with what we're doing – which tends to make us more successful.

So try it. Think of some buckets. If you're trying to save more, think about the different savings targets you have, and focus on how much you want each of them. If you are trying to develop your investing, think about buckets you want to invest in.

Grab a pen and paper and write down what you're saving towards: emergency fund, investment fund, retirement, freedom, even drawing them as buckets if you like. Visualise filling the buckets, and set targets for doing that. Turning cognitive biases to work in our favour can be a vital trick in moving towards personal finance success, and filling your buckets is a great way of doing that.

Step 12: Imbue

Today let's do a slower version of Step 9. Rather than noticing lots of things, let's notice one thing and give it more value. By spending time to appreciate that one thing, it will become more valuable to us.

Why is that important? Because too much of our spending is because we don't appreciate the things we already have. If we value what we already possess, we are less likely to try replacing it with something new.

This process can push back at the power of advertising which, if you think about it, is designed to imbue things we don't own with value. If a celebrity owns or uses something, we are supposed to think it is better than the thing we own or use. We can do the same, deliberately adding value to things we have.

If you like, you can select a specific item for this. If you want to start with a small easy step, pick something you already treasure: a photo of a favourite person, for example, or something they gave you. Allow yourself to think your most positive thoughts about this thing, and all the connections you have with it.

There is nothing wrong with possessions. There is nothing wrong with valuing things. But if we can spend our time to appreciate the things we have more than our money to acquire the things we don't, we can be free, in many meanings of the word, faster.

If you think that would be too easy, try to pick something that perhaps you don't value as directly.

On my desk, I have one thing I will use as an example: a drinking bottle. It is from the same company as one I used when a teenager and staying with a French family for one month in the Alps, and every weekend we would hike the local mountains. As we left the house, I would be handed a beaten-up old bottle that had seen much better days, but hours later, when I got to the top, cold water had never tasted so sweet. As a result, I bought myself a bottle by the same company when I got the chance, and although it isn't beaten up, and I am not up a mountain, it reminds me of those hikes.

Or at least it does now, while I am remembering it. Most of the time, it just sits there, ignored, all that value forgotten. I need to remind myself of its worth, its value, those connections.

Try the same process, giving thought to something you already have. It will make the things you don't have seem much less necessary.

Step 13: Degrees in Needs

When we were preparing *The Thousand Dollar Journal*, one migrant worker asked us to add a column to the spending tracker for her to tick whether the item was something she wanted or needed.

If that sounds like it makes sense to you, you can add the same thing to the zen spending tracker you made in Step 8.

You don't have to include it. For some people, separating between wants and needs is an unnecessary distraction. Should I think of everything more than my basic sustenance as a want? Or should I reflect that I want something because, at that moment, I feel like I need it?

What we don't need is judgement.

Instead, we can reflect if the thing we bought is needed more than we need our near-term financial peace of mind, or our longer-term financial freedom. We can reflect on whether the item kept us on our path, or took us off it. We can use the tracker to be honest with ourselves about our recent past.

If classifying between need and want, or "on the path" or "off" will help you, then add it to your zen tracker. On each day, you can jot down what you bought, how much it cost, and why. And how you feel about it. You can use any term you like to help you assess how you feel about that spending, if you thought it was worthwhile or not, and help you learn from it or not. And that's really what matters.

Step 14: Think About the Week

Did you make a notebook this week? If you didn't, please try. As we discussed, they're really two notebooks, one public and one hidden. If you like, that could be one for tracking and one for planning. One for observing and one for thinking. One for noticing, which I hope you were able to do more of, now you notice how often you do it.

Perhaps you can imbue this little piece of paper, which may have come off a stack in a printer tray, one of hundreds, with far more meaning than it could ever have had otherwise. Perhaps it can become a habit for you that develops meaning and value.

Take time over thinking about the week. I hope it was a good one. I hope thinking about it again can make it a little bit better.

Crawl

There is a zen buddhist belief that we are all born boddhisatvas, buddha-like beings in a state of bliss. It is the rigours of life, our emotions and struggles, that take us away from this state.

At the beginning of the movie *Finding Joe*, author Alan Cohen tells the story of a golden buddha hidden from invading armies in a layer of soil and dirt for so long that the locals forgot that it is golden underneath – until one day some of the cover chips off. Underneath it is all golden, as it was to begin with. Just like all of us.

This can feel hard to relate to about ourselves. We're so used to being hard on ourselves, as demanded by the outside world, that our layer of dirt can feel like it is concrete all the way down.

But if we remember some childhood joys, some of the simplest pleasures, we can feel its truth. Laughter could be easy.

Let's go back. Let's crawl before we walk.

Step 15: What Is It Like?

We rush to judge. We too hastily try to answer the question "Is this good or bad?" rather than asking "What is this like?"

We do it to things outside us, and we do it to ourselves. We do it when it is pointless and even harmful.

Our senses do not have those kinds of gradations. At the simplest level, we don't know if the volume is turned to 10 or 11 without looking at the dial. Or how hot things really are, or how blue. And yet we try to score a wine 17.5 out of 20, and a film 98 out of 100.

There is an exasperating stage of childhood, for parents, when babies stick everything that will fit into their chubby hands directly into their mouths. This is not done solely for the pleasure of watching their parents panic – although that does seem to happen in the latter part of this stage – but so they can really feel what this thing is like. While our hands have the most nerve endings of the outer parts of our bodies, our tongues have many, many more, and babies somehow know this. By putting the object into their mouths they are really feeling what the object is like.

They may subsequently decide the item is good ("mmm, biscuit") or bad ("carrot") but most objects aren't getting graded. The object is being assessed. They want to know what this thing is like.

No, don't start sticking everything in your mouth.

Just don't ask yourself whether things are good or bad. Don't rank anything between 1 and 10 unless it is asking to be ranked. Unless it is useful to do so. Ask yourself what it is like, and enjoy the process of rediscovering things.

Not judging doesn't mean not thinking about things. It just means not dismissing things between only two impossible to define characteristics of good or bad.

"Is this coffee good or bad?" isn't a question that's worth the price of the coffee. If it's a black coffee, you can ask yourself what aroma it has. A simple starting point is to ask yourself if it is stronger than usual. Does it have sour or acidic elements to it? Is the taste similar to the smell, or is it different?

If you look more deeply into the experience of experiencing something, you will get more from that experience. The experience can become good, even if the coffee isn't.

And that can make even a bad coffee better value for your money.

Step 16: Easy as Pie

If you've been tracking your spending for two weeks, you should have a collection of receipts and some scribbles on a notebook. Today is the day to pull them all together and add up what you're spending on. It may not be totally scientific, but if it's our first attempt, that is fine.

There's a theory suggesting that we should spend 50% of our income on essentials (rent, utilities, transport), 30% on enjoyment (you don't need me to tell you what that is), and save the remaining 20%.

Let's look at it another way, and change the numbers slightly. In a page of your zen tracker (or any other handy piece of paper), draw a circle. It doesn't have to be as artistic as a zen ensō, just a rough circle, and then divide it in half. Divide the right half into two again. You should now have a circle with two quarters on the right, and one half on the left.

Next to the top right quarter segment, write "Save". Saving comes first, remember? Next to the bottom right quadrant, write "Enjoy". Next to the big left half, write "Need".

How does the spending you have tracked so far match to this? Ask yourself if this 25/25/50 split is ideal for you. I switched it to that because it's easier to draw, but 5% extra savings can bring about financial freedom six years faster: worth it, I think.

Start using this simple pie chart to think about how you're allocating your money, and if that's where you want it to go. Let's not just think "spending bad, saving good", but make sure we are doing the best, the most interesting, the most valuable things with our money.

If you like, you can shade in a fourth section, between saved and enjoy, and label it "Waste". That's money spent that wasn't essential, you didn't enjoy much and could have been saved. If there's any of that during the week, that's some you can save next time instead.

Step 17: Crawl Before You Walk

Life feels so much better when we feel fit and healthy. It's easier to enjoy ourselves for free when our bodies are able to move without pain. Even just a little bit of pain, and it is so easy to think about spending some money to try to feel better – even though that rarely works for long.

The fitness industry knows this. It tries to sell us gym memberships, health supplements, subscription apps, and all kinds of other possible answers to our problem, and while our health is one of the best things we can spend our money on, these are so rarely the solution.

One reason is because they offer to take us to a place we aren't really ready to reach yet. We shouldn't be doing heavy weights before our core and stabiliser muscles are strong: we shouldn't run before we walk, and we shouldn't walk before we can crawl.

I mean it.

Crawl. On the ground. Hands and feet. Moving forward, moving backwards, moving side-to-side.

The basic crawls are often called "bear" and "tiger". They both involve crawling on hands and feet, one hand and foot moving forward at a time, with your body low for a tiger crawl, and your back and buttocks high for bear.

If you haven't done it since you were a baby, it will work your whole body, exhausting you, but it will do it in an incredibly low impact way, strengthening all your core, connective and stabilising tissue. It has some similarity to yoga without the long pauses that strain those of us with either an attention or flexibility deficit.

We crawl as babies because we don't know how to walk yet – and because we're building all those muscles. We're the same, we should be prepared to be the same, building our muscles for the path ahead.

Crawling doesn't need anything, not even a big space. You can do it by your bed. It doesn't need equipment, you don't need to change to do it, and it doesn't even take a lot of time: you might be tired in five minutes. And it's free, no gym membership required.

Try crawling today. We'll walk soon enough.

Step 18: What Else Could I Do?

We are all too familiar with the concept of FOMO, the fear of missing out that supposedly drives too many of us to do things we don't necessarily want to do.

But opportunity cost, which we could think of as the cost of missing out, or COMO, rarely gets a mention, despite being an important life-skill and investment skill.

Every choice requires turning down a different choice. Every fork in the path involves rejecting one, choosing the other. Everything we do with our money means we can't do something else. We should try to make sure we get the most value we can from it.

This is true for investing too, and it can be more obvious. If you are at the stage where you have started saving some money, and you have a savings account, do some research today to find an account that pays a higher return. If you are getting 1% on your money, see if you can get 1.5%. Or maybe even 2%. Look around for a new option. If the risk is the same between the two savings accounts, this is now your opportunity cost. You could get higher returns.

It might not sound like a big difference, but this is how we develop our investment skills. Just like we can't run before walking and crawling, we can't successfully go from a savings account to options trading. There are steps in between, and the incremental essence of those steps is understanding our opportunity cost.

If you already have an investment account, and you're investing in a large safe index, you could consider a different one, one that favours a specific sector (technology or green energy), or different countries.

Ask yourself "What return am I getting today, and what would be the next small improvement, for not much extra risk? Or get the same return, for less risk?"

Make it small, make it comfortable, but ask the question. Unlike a fork in the path, where we have to choose one or the other, you can put a small amount of money in your new choice, testing it out.

What else could you do? Take a deep breath and find a new investment today.

Step 19: Triangular Breathing

Today, let's try some breathing techniques in different shapes, starting with a triangle.

The way our brains and bodies connect via our nervous system is too complicated for me to explain, because I am not an expert and I don't have space. What I do know is that when we control our breathing, and hold that breath, either with air in our lungs or out of our lungs, it affects our nervous system in different ways. Some affect the way we consciously control our nervous system, and some the way we subconsciously do it.

I also know that getting good at breathing is one of the fastest and cheapest ways of feeling much better. So if we want financial peace of mind, we should try to get good at this.

Obviously, most breathing is just in and out. When we don't think about our breathing, it can become quite shallow. If we suffer from mild stress, it can become shallower and more constrained: we don't get enough oxygen, we build up carbon dioxide, and our blood can become more acidic as a result.

The first change we can make to the shape of our breathing is to make it triangular. This can involve holding our breath in our lungs, which is easy, or holding our breath out of our lungs, which requires a bit more thought. Let's do that.

Count to four while you're breathing in, steadily, so it takes roughly four seconds. Count to seven while you're breathing out, same count. Before you breathe in again, count to eight. Do this a few times.

This breathing pattern, based on yogic pranayama breathwork, was popularised by Dr Andrew Weil, who called it a natural tranquilizer for the body, as holding empty lungs has a powerful calming effect on our stress systems.

Try it now. 4 - 7 - 8. 4 - 7 - 8. 4 - 7 - 8.

Repeat it up to ten times, and then scan your thoughts around your body, to see how it feels, if you can sense any changes. You might feel some tingles, or extra calmness or coolness. Just from a minute of breathing.

Practice this until you're comfortable with doing it. Practice on the bus, or at your desk at work, at home on the couch or in bed. Any time you might want to feel a little more relaxed, like when you're uncertain about whether to spend money or not.

Step 20: Take A Picture

You see something in a shop you know a friend of yours would like, and maybe find it a bit funny, although they may not need to actually own it.

There was a time when you would have had three choices. Buy it for your friend, drag your friend there on your next trip, or feel the frustration of wanting to do something and not be able to do it.

Now you don't have to do that. You can take a picture of it and send it to them. Done. No frustration.

What about doing that for yourself?

If you see something you like, just take a photo of it.

The act of buying often releases the frustration that browsing shops can generate. We see something we like – we have to buy it. If we don't, we'll feel frustrated, or perhaps sad and stressed.

Taking the photograph can replace the act of purchasing and remove the stress hormones and emotions from our system. We can accompany it with a thought to tell our friend later. Or to look at it later if we want to think about it ourselves.

We may remember, we may forget, because we have overcome the stress of that moment. But we will feel better, and we will still have our money!

Step 21: How Does This Feel?

Take some time to assess how you feel about the practices so far.

Breathe a little, think about your money, plan your investing, maybe crawl on the floor. Notice which makes you feel stronger, or which has no impact.

It is ok. We all need slightly different paths. In the next week we will pick up the pace, stop crawling and start walking.

Maybe today is a good day to get ready and make a little notebook for the week ahead. If you haven't written any spending down recently, go back to that habit now, and journal your expenditure alongside your thoughts about it.

Learning is a tricky thing. Things that can seem simple to some people can be tough to impossible to others: the difference often isn't about intelligence, but about the foundations the learning is built on.

If you really understood everything before a new idea, you will probably be able to get your head around the next bit. If you were a bit wobbly on some of the earlier ideas, the next one could make the whole thing fall down.

Now is a good time to assess where you are on your learning path, and how wobbly that knowledge is.

If you get lost when walking, the smartest thing to do is go back to the last place you were certain you knew where you were. The same thing with learning too. Go back to where you're 100% certain.

If that's with having a savings account, and putting money on deposit, that's great. If you're saving an emergency fund, that's where your money needs to go.

But that's also a good point to start learning about what you should do next, and get ready for that step. For most people, that will be investing in index funds. If you find the concept of index investing a little confusing, start with finding out what index funds are available to you: you should be able to find a way of investing in something that tracks the S&P 500. Learn how to do that, and how to do it with the lowest cost possible. You will then be ready for the practical step of investing in an index when your emergency fund is full.

Take time to know where you are in your path, and if you are comfortable with it. If you aren't, go back to the level before and learn as much as you can.

Sometimes, once you step back, you might need to take a baby step to become more comfortable, so a small investment will make you feel more confident. Think about how you could do that, and where it will be most relevant.

Don't just think you can rush along the path all in one go. Understand that the path will take time, and know where you are.

For today's exercise, work out where in your financial knowledge you are most comfortable, where you are less comfortable, and find information that will help you make small steps between those two points.

Walk

Many of the steps on our path aren't really about the money.

Walking a path to financial peace of mind only has money as a very small component of it. Our general peace of mind, and how we use it to approach money, will have a very important role to play. And is more important than money.

The next seven steps are the middle seven in our little guide to the start of the path. Most of them have nothing to do with money. They are about thought, breath, goals, life.

Please try them and enjoy them.

Step 22: Sit. Walk. Don't Wobble

We have discussed before how valuable our attention is. The bizarre little mantra above, which comes from a zen Buddhist tradition, conveys that importance in four short words. When you're sitting, just sit. When you're walking, just walk. Don't think about other stuff when you're doing something: happiness lies in focus.

In his book *Flow: The Psychology of Optimal Experience*, Mihaly Csikszentmihalyi makes a similar, if more detailed point. He claims that flow states, when we almost totally lose the sense of our surroundings, including our thoughts and worries about the rest of our lives, because we are so absorbed by what we are doing, can become so enjoyable as to be almost addictive – but they come through the hard work of focus.

Sit, walk, flow.

Please try it today. Right now, you're reading this. If you're reading this while doing something else (Is the TV on? Is your phone nearby? Are you eating lunch?), pick one of those things and just do that. And only do that. Don't think about anything else.

Perhaps you can try it right now with the simplest: breathing.

Because it's the simplest, it is also the hardest: there's less going on to focus on, so our distractions can be noisier. That's perhaps why it is the starting point of so many meditation practices.

Stop reading now, set a timer for five minutes, and just think about your breathing. Sit, walk, breathe, flow.

Step 23: Go for A Walk

Do any of us go for too many walks? Obviously not, and if none of us are going for too many walks, it's likely that most of us aren't going for enough.

Some of us may feel we walk too much, but that's not the same. That's walking to somewhere: work, the shops, an appointment at the dentist. That's walking as a form of transport. Not a walk.

Go for a walk and enjoy it.

I feel there are three ways of really enjoying going for a walk on your own. Obviously a walk with good company is a great thing too, but it relies on the company. A walk on your own is just that, and can be wonderful.

The easiest way to enjoy it is without a set route, and without a set way of thinking about the walk: just ramble, letting your feet and your mind take you wherever they want to go. Your thoughts can run wild, even if your shoes just pound the pavement. Each turn could lead to a new place, or a new idea. Run, or rather, walk with it.

Then there is a more intentional walk. Set out knowing the route you will take, and decide you want to think about a particular thing. It could be planning an event, or deciding between two investments. Bring some way of making notes – your folded zen tracker notebook will be perfect. You could instead choose to walk and notice more: engage your mind in its surroundings. Plan to see more, look for more, have the intention to focus on what is going on around you. All of these work.

The toughest walk is to think about walking itself, Thich Nhat Hanh-style, "arriving with every step". I suggest you make this a short walk, it's too hard to keep up over any kind of distance. One foot goes in front of another. Your arms move. Do your hips sway? Gently or widely? Your foot lands and rolls, heel to toe – or does it?

Try to use the same level of focus you would give your body if it were tired, when muscles would be complaining, joints aching, blisters forming on your heels, but do it without the pain, with enjoyment. Look around your body as you walk.

See if you can get as far as the shops, or wherever is the closest landmark you can pick out, without thinking about anything else. Good luck.

Step 24: Box Breathing

Let's breathe differently today. We've counted to ten while breathing, and we've taken triangular breaths. Today, let's do square breaths, or box breathing.

Perhaps start by counting to three as you breathe in. Then hold your breath in your lungs as you count to three, breathe out as you count to three, and then pause for three seconds before breathing in again.

Easy? Try counting to four at each stage of the process, while remembering this isn't a competition. You don't get more points for counting to 12 at each stage than you do for counting to four. You don't get any points at all – and in fact, the people who can't get to six may be getting more benefits at five than someone who can skip right past it.

Mark Divine, a US Navy Seal who has helped popularise the concept, claims he used it every day in training to deal with stressful situations, to help his body purge the chemicals and hormones that can otherwise sit in our system after we are stressed.

It's important to practice doing it before we are stressed though. To see how, even on a nice calm day, it can make us feel better.

So whichever day it is today, calm or stressed, try it now: inhale, pause, exhale, pause.

Do it for at least 10 cycles if you can, or even for as long as five minutes, and then see how you feel. Enjoy.

Step 25: Because You're Worth It!

I dislike the phrase "net worth", as it confuses money and value. All of us, all humans, and from a Buddhist perspective, all living beings, are worth so much more than money, that "net worth" can feel demeaning.

But it is a useful exercise to calculate what the financial value is of all your assets, minus all your liabilities. Put more simply, if you had to sell everything you own today, and pay back all your debts, do you know how much you would have left?

If you don't, it's a good exercise to practice, because one day, you want this total to be 25× your annual spending (300× your monthly spending), so, as with any path, it's good to know how far you have to go to the end.

It can also be a very simple exercise. If you have one, two or three types of investments, add up the totals of those:

Assets equal: "X in my cash account, Y in my savings account, Z in my investment fund."

You can write that down now in your little zen tracker, and add up the total.

Then what do you owe? If you don't have any debt at all, then what spending have you already planned to take out of those totals?

Liabilities equal: "A on my credit card, B to pay for my holiday in July." Add those up, and then take it away from the first number, your assets.

This is your current financial net worth.

You are worth much more than this, obviously, and one day your financial net worth will be larger too, but know where the end of your path lies, and where you are on it today.

Step 26: Wobble!

I have one very wobbly practice. I know the mantra says don't wobble, but I do this wobble deliberately, so I think it is ok.

You're going to laugh at me for this, but when I brush my teeth in the morning, I do it standing on one foot. On tiptoe. And I wobble. A lot.

That's because the main focus of the practice wasn't about meditation, it was about strengthening my calf muscles after a knee injury. I knew I needed to run in a way where my feet struck the ground further forward, but this put a strain on my calves, and so they needed strengthening.

In his book *The Cool Impossible*, Eric Orton outlines training your feet, ankles, heels and calves to be stronger by standing on one foot, on tiptoe, on a slant or wobble board. It seemed to work, but I struggled to fit this short extra practice into the rest of my training until one morning, staring at myself in the mirror as I brushed my teeth, I realised I could do it right there and then.

I don't use a wobble or slant board for this (it's ridiculous enough already!), but I do it every day, and have been doing it for almost two years. In my head I have a theory that it not only makes my lower legs stronger, it improves my balance, which may help to stop me falling: when I run, and when I get older.

It also requires me to focus on my body first thing in the morning: balancing isn't just about your feet and legs, your upper body will sway too. Some days, I need to focus a lot on just how my body feels. Other days, I get distracted and think about the day ahead, which often results in me getting even wobblier.

Do you want to try it? I assume you plan on brushing your teeth some time in the next 24 hours, so there's an opportunity then.

You have my permission to wobble.

Step 27: Give Yourself Permission

One of the cleverest things marketing does is give us permission to do things. Marketing knows we are told not to do things since childhood, told we shouldn't do this, shouldn't do that: and it knows we all privately rebel against this feeling.

So if marketing tells us we have permission to do something, we feel released, and we do it.

Unfortunately, the thing they normally give us permission to do is to spend money on the thing they're selling, which is often something we don't really need. We get so much of this permission every minute of every day, that we eventually listen to some of it, and buy something we don't value as much as the money we had, and so we tell ourselves we shouldn't do that in future.

But that feeling of "shouldn't" becomes something we feel we should rebel against again, and so the cycle repeats.

We already discussed how the inventor of modern marketing changed the world by encouraging American women to smoke by telling them it would show their liberation from men who insisted they shouldn't smoke as it is unladylike. It is that powerful.

We can use that power for ourselves, though. We can give ourselves permission. You can find something you have been telling yourself you shouldn't do, you're embarrassed to do, and do it anyway.

Like my wobbling, which I find embarrassing to admit, and you may be embarrassed to follow. Give it a try. No one needs to see or know.

Or making the little eight-page book and tracking your spending. Or taking 10 breaths. Or breathing for five minutes. Or opening a savings account.

Is a feeling, an emotion, a thought, holding you back from doing something? It might have twisted the restriction into not liking, not having the energy, not feeling right for it. Think about it a little harder. Think about which of the last

26 steps you feel you are least likely to do, and then give yourself permission to do it.

If it helps you, imagine me giving you the permission. Imagine your family and friends giving you the permission. Give yourself permission to change.

Step 28: Look Back Down the Path

Are you comfortable where you are on the path as practice?

If not, you can choose to go back a bit, to become comfortable. Revisit past steps and enjoy them, enjoy doing them the second or third time, knowing what you're doing. The practice can be more important than the path.

Or you can push forward, giving yourself the permission to feel uncomfortable, or even a little wobbly, knowing you can go back whenever you like.

Repeat some of these most recent steps. Go for a walk. Calculate the value of your assets. Wobble.

You Might Be Wrong

In his book, *Wabi Sabi*, artist, musician and author Nobuo Suzuki explains that when seeking the truth "what you need to do, above all else, is to recognise you might be wrong".

This is not the same as constantly living in doubt, being so uncertain as to move forward.

You can move forward, expecting to be in roughly the right direction, but know you will occasionally need to change course a little, or walk back a couple of steps and get back on the right path for you.

This is reality.

Step 29: Write This Down

I hope you have been reviewing your spending, either every evening or every few days, to keep track of where your money goes. While it seems a new app to help you do this is launched every minute, there is a lot to be said for writing with pen and paper, even in our folded little notebooks.

Professor Audrey van der Meer of the Norwegian University of Science and Technology has run multiple studies to show how writing by hand develops more synapse and neuron activity than typing. In short, our brains become more active and this creates more ways for us to think about what we're doing, and then remember it.

There's even a school of thought that says you don't really know what you think about a subject until you write it down.

That's what I would love for you to try this week: think out loud on paper. Try a free-writing assignment, or two, and just scribble, scrawl, doodle, note, and think on to a sheet of paper what comes to mind.

No one is going to mark this. No one is going to know. You can save it for yourself if you want to note it down, or you can throw it away if you never want to see it again.

If you want to try immediately, go and find some writing materials.

Right now, before you read down to see the prompt. Ah-ah-ah. No cheating.

Anyway, we'll delay that for a second, and give you another chance. You can also set yourself a timer, perhaps just five minutes, to really ensure the writing you do is fresh and not over-thought. That's the point. No finely crafted essays allowed. We want to see our innermost thoughts.

So get a way of timing, and writing, and paper, and write down what financial peace of mind will mean to you.

Go.

Step 30: Who Have I Become?

I hear myself saying this little mantra when I find myself falling prey to advertising, pushing me to think I have become someone who needs the finer things in life, whether they are things I think I can afford or not.

"Who have I become that I need to buy this?"

I sometimes remember the description, fictionalised of course, that Steven Pressfield gives in his novel *The Virtues of War* of when Alexander the Great's troops meet the Greek philosopher Diogenes, asking him to stand aside as Alexander has conquered the known world. Diogenes reply? "I have conquered my need to conquer the world."

Conquering your need for shows of status is better than status. Conquering your need for comfort is better than comfort. Seeing the world as it really is, and fitting yourself to it, is better than distorting your view of it so that you can feel better.

You could start out by asking if you already have an area of spending that you're not proud of, that isn't who you want to become. It could be anything, ranging from addictions like drinking or smoking, to obsessing about gaming. It could be collecting sneakers or shoes, or constantly picking up new fads before dropping them.

It's ok. We all have something.

If you know you have one of these habits, and it is costing you money you would rather not spend, the first and most important stage is to admit it. Just admit it. "I wish I didn't spend so much money on . . ." and say its name.

You can write the sentence down too, to make it more memorable. You can get in the habit of doodling it. You can say to yourself, "I want to become the person who doesn't spend so much money on . . ."

This may be a long road. There may be easier wins first, giving up smaller items you know you can do easily. You may need to work out that there is a certain amount of this you "need" to be happy, to not feel like you are sacrificing too much. But you may feel that you can slowly increase the test, and become stronger as a result.

But you must always make the focus something positive. You are not giving up. You are gaining. Diogenes wasn't scared. He had conquered his need to conquer the world.

Step 31: Zero-Risk Fallacy

If you don't already have any investments, I want you to make that big step today. If you already have some, but they are small and very low risk, I want you to take a slightly larger risk today. It's important to take on some bigger risks – not huge ones, but sensible ones – as without risks, we won't get sufficient returns on our investments.

One of the things that keeps us back from investing is thinking it's too risky, or even worse, that we would rather have no risk at all.

This can be an example of a cognitive bias called "zero-risk bias", where we feel we only want to take the opportunity that has zero risks – without recognising that that is just not possible. There is no such thing as zero risk.

But the bias stems from not having a number approach to risk. Instead, many of us have an emotional approach to it. Something feels risky because we know less about it, and so we get a nervous feeling about it in our guts. Is that nervous feeling a 7 or a 9? Who can say?! But we just want it to go away, and so we decide not to take the risk at all. No risk, no emotion – but also no investment.

The reality is that risk is part and parcel of investing, and a sensible investment portfolio will have a wide spread of different risks, some small, offering lower returns, some big, having potential for huge returns, some hopefully non-correlated, so they will go up when other things go down. That's how to manage risk, not by hiding from it and hoping for zero risk.

So open your investment account today, and invest in something new. If you've not invested in an index before, try that today. Start.

Step 32: Breathe the Ocean

This "ocean cave" is possibly my favourite breathing technique. I think of it as having a shape, like the triangular and box breathing we have started doing, even though the actual breathing is just straight in, straight out, as deep as I can make it.

It needs a bit of a warm-up. Here's what you do.

Lie down, close your eyes and start breathing, slow and relaxed. Take stock of your body, make sure it feels relaxed all over: feet, fingers, arms, shoulders, legs, back, everywhere.

Once that's done, start picking up the depth of your breathing. On an exhale, fully breathe out, expelling as much air from your lungs as you can without it tensing your body. Now, as you breathe in, imagine the air filling first the lower parts of your stomach first, and then the inflation moves up your body, to your upper stomach, your lower chest, your upper chest, and almost to your shoulders. Your whole abdomen should have slowly pulsated up, from just above your hips to right below your neck.

Then breathe out, in the reverse order, relaxing your shoulders, upper ribs, upper and lower abs, until you've breathed out all of that air, nice and slowly. You might be able to do a count of roughly 10 or 15 seconds for the inhalation, and the same for exhaling, although the timing isn't important.

Do this a few times. Get used to the rhythm, the flow of the air and body, moving up and in, down and out.

You can imagine your body being an ocean cave as the tide rushes in. The air you breathe in can feel like a cold wave pushing and foaming into the mouth of the cave, moving up, splashing against the walls, filling it right into the very end of the cave, before the wave recedes, pulls back all the way into the ocean, leaving the cave empty, sparklingly clean.

Each breath is a new wave, a new opportunity to clean up what was there before.

The waves might even push beyond your shoulders, you might feel them crashing around in a new cave chamber in your head. Although you can't breathe there, obviously, you can often feel the pressure in your head from a very deep breath, and that could become an even deeper wave, cleaning even further, even deeper, before washing out to sea.

Sometimes the waves can be relatively calm, and other times they can rush in with impressive force. After a while, I can't help but feel that the walls of the cave – me – have been washed clean by this remorseless action. I have no idea if it has any scientific benefits at all, I just find it enjoyable and calming. I find it makes it easier to breathe more deeply – and that can't be bad.

Step 33: Mindful Screen Use

We all know we need a little more freedom from digital distraction, but we also know we need to fight for it.

Some people fight by keeping their phones in the living room when they're in the bedroom, or in the bedroom when they're in the living room. You can't reach for it, even if you want to.

Some people go for digital detoxes, starting by leaving their phone at home when going for a walk. Others are even brave enough to go on holiday without them. How does that feel?

Others go the digital versus digital approach, turning off all reminders, notifications, pings, and banners. I wish somehow I could persuade social media to make my thumb ache when I scroll down a feed for more than a few seconds. . . .

Our focus and attention are so important that whatever strategy works for you, then please go for it. We need every tool in the box for this one.

My personal favourite is to develop mindfulness with picking up my devices, resisting the desire to pick the phone up whenever I feel like it.

I have a confession to make: I am the person who eats all the chocolate in the house. I don't buy it, because when I am in the supermarket, I don't really like chocolate. When it's in the fridge, though, I love it. And so I eat it all.

I am the same with the phone. Once I pick it up, I could be there all day, immediately forgetting why I had picked it up, but like a dog in a thicket, hunting down interesting new tracks and scents, one a second. There's always something else there.

But I don't have to pick it up. It's fine. It can stay there. As long as I don't pick it up, I feel I can do other more interesting things. It might be something as mindless as watching television in a more engaged way, or it might be writing this section undisturbed without looking up a website about digital attention spans.

We need something to make it positive though, and so sometimes I count. When I am in the mood, I count the number of times in a row I have looked at my phone and thought about picking it up, and not done it, and then got back to doing something else. Sometimes I write it down, most often I forget, but it gives me enough reason to resist for a while, and be mindful for a little longer.

Step 34: Mindful Spending

In *WabiSabi*, Nobuo Suzuki explains the two main reasons he owned things before giving up a consumerist lifestyle and adopting a zen way of life.

"If I have newer and better stuff, everything will be better. If I have all this, others will value me more."

When Suzuki realised that he was thinking this way, and that neither statement was true, he decided to throw away most of his possessions and live a much simpler life.

We don't have to do the same, but we can recognise his feelings. We all know that neither statement is true, and we all know that we have these feelings, those same emotions, gnawing at our stomachs if not written out as honestly as he did.

Today, if you do any shopping, try to bring some real zen mindfulness to the purchase. Ask yourself deeply if it is something that you will use, something you will need, something that will add to your existence.

This doesn't have to take joy from shopping. The opposite can be true. You can do what we are supposed to do in shops, and reject 99.9999999% of all the items, as they won't change our lives. We can buy the things that sustain us and give us real joy.

We don't need to aim for 100% success at this. Just pausing as we search is enough. Just recognising that we are buying, acknowledging what we are doing, and asking the right question is the improvement we are looking for.

We are looking to be "in the moment" of shopping: that does not mean being lost in the reverie of lights, advertising, and promotions. It means knowing what we are doing, while we are doing it.

Step 35: Where Are You?

Have you begun saving? Have you begun investing? Are you sending money from your current account to your investment account as soon as you can?

Are you keeping track of your spending better than you ever have before? Can you still do better?

Assess where you are on the path right now. This book is only going to provide 14 more steps, and some of them are deliberately challenging. If you would like some easier ones, I would suggest you go back along the early steps of The Path Is Practice and find some areas that you can strengthen before proceeding.

Remember, being on a path, and knowing where you are going, is more important than going fast without direction.

Know where you are.

Challenges

I hope you've enjoyed the steps so far. Some of them are designed to be really easy, some of them a little bit more of a stretch – but not the next seven. The next seven are all designed to be a challenge.

That's because you have more in you that you will only discover when you push yourself. What you can do today, you only know because you tried something for the first time before. You don't know if you can or can't do the things you haven't tried.

That's why these challenges are here. You may already have tried some of them before, and not found them tough. You may never have wanted to do some of them – please do try. This is how we find out about ourselves.

Step 36: No Spend Days

We all need to spend some money, it's true. We need food, rent, heat. But many of us also spend lots of money that is really unnecessary. One way to find out how much that can be is to set ourselves a no-spending challenge, in which we don't spend anything beyond some set parameters.

Start with a day: see if you can spend no money at all for 24 hours. Groceries are normally allowed in these challenges, but it's actually better to have bought them in advance. Plan what you're going to need – but also make sure you plan what you're going to go without. No eating out or drinking. No cabs. No "shopping".

If a day turns out to be easy, challenge yourself to see how long you can go on for. Weekdays? Into the weekend? Some people manage to push for entire "no spend months".

The point is two-fold. One, this is a wonderful exercise in mindfulness and discipline, having control over your surroundings rather than being pushed around by impulse.

Two, it should turbo-boost your savings. At the end of the challenge, calculate how much extra you think you've saved by "no spending", and then pop that into your investment account.

Win-win.

Step 37: Fast Gains

What if you didn't eat for 24 hours? Well, you definitely wouldn't be spending money on food, at least!

Fasting is a part of many monastic traditions, perhaps because it is healthy, but also perhaps because it asks us to recognise that the "comfort" of just eating when we want to, is giving in to another easy temptation, and we might have better self-awareness if we don't.

Being genuinely hungry is nothing to joke about, but many of us are at least days away from real hunger if we don't eat. Our bodies have become used to three or even more meals a day, and so cutting back to two meals, or one, or even none, can be a real education about how our bodies react.

We will sometimes feel hunger pangs, but it can be surprising how quickly they pass. We might also sometimes feel a little light-headed, but that isn't necessarily a sensation of weakness but our bodies burning fuel we're not used to them burning.

There are increasing numbers of studies that show fasting has all kinds of health benefits for our bodies and minds: the kinds of benefits we would otherwise need to pay a fortune for in medication or in health farms, but that we can replicate for nothing. Literally, nothing.

Perhaps all we need is a zen state of mind. If we cultivate a desire to fast for 24 hours, to see how our body feels, how it copes, how it pushes through, then it will be much easier.

If you have a dietary or digestive condition that you think might not benefit from fasting, please check with your doctor (not the internet) before proceeding with this.

Otherwise, decide when and what your last meal will be, and what you will allow to pass your lips during your fast. I drink water, some coffee, and some tea.

Enjoy.

Step 38: Breathe

I felt blessed to be introduced to Chun in Singapore. Chun has trained with Wim "The Iceman" Hof himself, climbing a Polish mountain in shorts and little else, and learning multiple deep breathing and ice bathing techniques.

Prior to meeting Chun, I had watched some of Wim Hof's videos online. I was already convinced by the ice baths (it's not easy to have an ice bath in Singapore – as the three chest freezers on Chun's balcony demonstrate) but struggled to really establish a good rhythm with the breathing exercises. Perhaps it was trying to watch a video while closing my eyes, or set a timer, or other distractions.

A couple of sessions with Chun and I was set straight, and more comfortable to play with Wim Hof style breathing.

In essence, Wim Hof's quick but fairly deep brea-thing style, particularly with an emphasis on the exhalation part of the cycle more than the inhalation, helps clear the blood stream of CO_2. What that does is alkalise your blood, which can reduce pain (think Lamaze breathing techniques), lower inflammation, and bring about a profound sense of relaxation.

If you want to try it right now, lie down, close your eyes and take about 30 breaths. They can be quite quick, not overly shallow though, and you should fully breathe out on the exhale. After the 30th, take a deep breath in, breathe out all the way, and then don't worry about breathing in again until you really, really feel the need. That could be a minute later. Maybe more. Repeat that same cycle a few times, and you might find you don't need to breathe in again for two or three minutes, and you'll feel incredibly relaxed while doing so.

There are lots of Wim Hof videos on Youtube, and an increasing number of Spotify tracks that you can breathe along to as well. Try it and you'll perhaps find a way of quickly boosting your peace of mind that you can use at any time.

NOTE: This can be deadly anywhere near water. You can become so relaxed as to pass out, which is fine lying down on dry land, not anywhere near water. Don't do it.

Step 39: Work for Free

One of the most powerful things you can do in life is help other people. It can be powerful for them, and just as powerful for you.

We know that some people are better at team endeavours than they are at individual sports. Something about playing for others, not letting their side down, motivates them to try harder, to push further, to strive that little bit more.

Try that this week. Become a part of something bigger. You could clean a beach or a river, visit some old people in a care home, help a charity sort clothes or a food bank collect unwanted items. There are so many possibilities.

What will this achieve? For the people you are helping, you may think you aren't doing much. Perhaps a few bags of plastic litter cleaned from a river near you might not seem like much, but that waste might otherwise have been there a hundred or a thousand years. You've made the world better.

Perhaps you will help collect a child's coat that will one day be given to a family in need, and it will keep that child warm, making her day.

You will probably never know the full benefits your work for others will have, and for whom, but you can feel very quickly the benefits it will have for you.

It will probably introduce you to new people, good people who are helping others. This can be life-affirming. It can tell you that you are doing good things, which can be self-affirming. It may give you a sense of achievement you aren't getting in your day job.

These are all things money can't buy, which often means we feel less inclined to buy things. We will already be happier, so the marketing tactic of making us feel insecure won't work so well.

In addition, you will have a new perspective. If you're helping people with low or no income, more of your spending will seem pointless. If you're helping clean the planet, more of your spending will seem polluting.

Plus, volunteering is generally free, so that's an activity that doesn't cost anything. Please try it as a challenge.

Step 40: Read Another Little Book

Now you're near the end of this little book, I would like you to get ready to read another one: *The Little Book of Common Sense Investing* by John C. Bogle.

Mr Bogle's advice has changed the way millions of people invest across the world. Much of our ability to invest at low-cost is due to the work of the company he founded, Vanguard, which created reliable structures for people to invest in at much lower fees.

If you've never read an investment book before, and have been put off by jargon, complexity or bravado, you should by this stage of this book feel a little more comfortable, understanding what you need to achieve from it, and Mr Bogle's work will be the next best place to head.

We could perhaps sum up the book in one phrase: "Don't look for the needle in the haystack. Just buy the haystack!" The great thing is, Jack Bogle not only provided proof that this was best (to continue his analogy, buying the haystack has delivered 9.6% returns over the long-term, looking for the needle has only delivered 0.1%!), he created structures that helped us all to buy the haystack affordably.

Reading his book will provide a wonderful description of the next section of your path, and perhaps even your entire path to financial peace of mind.

Yes, we know buying this book will cost money, and we don't often recommend spending money, but this is a book that is definitely worth it.

Step 41: Push Yourself to Breaking Point

The whole point of the challenges we've already listed has been to push yourself a little bit further. Don't spend. Don't eat. Help others.

I want you to think of one more for yourself, something aligned with our goals of achieving financial peace of mind, but that you know you're not willing to take on.

I'll give you an example. Perhaps you've struggled with some of the breathing and meditation exercises so far: perhaps a real challenge for you would be a one-hour meditation.

Maybe you are not really into exercise, so going for a three-hour walk would exhaust you: that could be your challenge.

The point is this: you can do more than you think. Every year, millions of people run marathons for the first time having thought they were the kind of people who couldn't.

It doesn't matter if they finish and swear to themselves they're never doing it again, because they have taught themselves something far more important than running. They have taught themselves they can push themselves further than they previously imagined.

You can too.

As we approach the end of the 49 steps we're providing to start your path to financial peace of mind, this is important. The end of that path can look a long way off, beyond the horizon, and it might be tempting to stop.

But you can get there, you can achieve things you thought you couldn't.

So imagine a challenge of your own that will really stretch you, write it down in your little zen notebook and commit to it now.

Even if you try and fail, if you meditate for 30 minutes and not a full hour, or walk for two hours and not three, it isn't a failure if you tried. You will have built muscles you didn't have before, and you will know more work needs to be done.

Step 42: Analyse Your Finances

If you're comfortable with a spreadsheet, pull up an empty Excel or Google sheet file and do this there. If not, or if this is the first time you've done this, a sheet of A4 paper (or maybe two) will do nicely.

First, obviously, savings. Write down your total savings, investments, assets, minus any debt (mortgage) against them.

Now write down how much you're currently saving every month. You may have been following these new steps for a month or more now, so you may have been able to save a little more.

And now your spending. What has your spending been for the last couple of months? Write it down.

Multiply that monthly spending number by 300. Write down your most recent monthly spending total, multiply it by three and then add two zeroes at the end. That's roughly your target for total financial freedom.

Subtract the total savings, investments, and assets you calculated in #1 from your target for total financial freedom. That's how far along the path you have to go. It could be a long way, I know, but this is where we begin, at the beginning.

Can you divide the total target minus your current savings by your monthly saving amount? That's how many months you have to save to get to your target.

If you don't invest. You must invest.

Returns of 7% will double every 10 years, and what you save today will have increased by eight times in 30 years.

With this information, find the Freedom Formula Calculator on the Start Investing Now page on www .sevendollarmillionaire.com. In summary, if you're saving

10% of your income, and you have no savings, it could take 55 years to hit that number. If you're saving 25%, 34 years. If 50%, 17 years.

There are two challenges here.

First, doing the numbers. None of those calculations is difficult in itself, but there's a sequence of them, and doing them one after another will make it more possible.

Second, not being scared by the numbers. Once you're done, the task may seem insurmountable. Saving and investing for freedom is something that takes years, often decades. You can accelerate it, if you choose, but you can also work steadily towards it. Remember, this is a path on a very long journey: each step, one after another, will get you there.

That's what paths are. One day, you will be able to look back at this step and remember, either how your life has improved since or how it hasn't. While it isn't entirely up to you, some of it will be.

The Journey

"A good traveller has no fixed plans and is not intent on arriving."

—*Lao Tzu*

We believe there is a path to financial peace of mind. The end of that path might be financial freedom, or it might not. It is also important, perhaps more valuable, that the path itself provides certainty, so we can live with more contentment.

As Nietsche said, "Not every end is the goal. The end of a melody is not its goal, and yet if a melody has not reached its end, it has not reached its goal."

For the final practice ideas, we are going to repeat the MISSION steps, to remind ourselves of the landmarks on the journey, but also to remember that this is all they are. They are not stages in a race, but they are guides to know how comfortable we are becoming in our relationship with money.

Step 43: Money and the Door

Money is a tool. Money is time and energy, creativity, inspiration, and skill. Money is many things.

Money is not emotion, though. It has none and it can give none to us – but we have become used to attaching feelings to it, so that we think it can.

If we are contemplating buying something we really like, that's very expensive, but we know we can't afford, we can imagine the joy we might feel once we own this thing. Even though we know the joy would diminish almost immediately, perhaps even as soon as we walk out of the shop.

Have you ever gone into a room to get something and forgotten why? It's actually a studied psychological phenomenon, called the doorway effect, where our memories suffer as we walk through a door. Apparently, our brains know as they enter a room that they are going to need space for a lot of new information, and so they get rid of a bunch of old data, clearing out our short-term memory.

It's useful for doing new tasks, not so great for remembering what we came here for.

We can use this to our advantage. Whenever you feel your emotions connecting to money, imagining a purchase making you happy, walk out of the door. It could be a real door, like the one to the street from the fancy shop you are in, or just opening a new app on your phone.

Your memory will clear a little, and your emotions will adjust. You may realise the right thing to do is keep on walking along the street and put the money in the bank instead.

Today's task: use the doorway to forget about spending and get on the path to financial peace of mind.

Step 44: Cut Out the Income Middle Man

Yes, it's great to earn more money, but it isn't the only way to be happier. Far from it.

The meaning of the word, income, as we discussed before, is about getting some money to come in to our lives, which we can then use to structure our saving, investing, and spending to optimise for our long-term happiness.

But what if we could work for long-term happiness directly instead? *The Journal of Happiness* reported in 2020 that people who did some form of volunteer work every month were happier than people who didn't. This was no quick and easy study, but reflected 70,000 respondents over more than 10 years, and also corrected for whether the kind of people who volunteer are happier anyway. And the answer is no: it's all about volunteering.

Doing some form of work to help others could cut out the middle man of money, and buy you some genuine happiness. Remembering the example of my friend Nick Thompson, beach-cleaning in Hong Kong, we know it provides eudonic happiness, the kind that sticks around for the long-term.

Today's task: find something you would love to volunteer for, and contact them.

Step 45: Saving Is an Action

One of the key reasons people who have enough money to save don't do it is because it can feel passive. While spending money feels active, saving feels like "not spending" and therefore passive.

Reverse this. Make saving an action. Put the money into a place you want to keep it. Choose a new investment vehicle. Add new money to your existing savings, and note how much it has increased.

This is action.

This is important. The only reason "retail therapy" works in the very short term is that action removes the cortisol hormone that builds up when our system is under stress. Any action will remove it: a walk, for example.

Make saving money an action and it will do the same thing, but the stress will be removed for longer, because you will not experience any buyer's remorse. You will still have the money, after all.

It is why we always put saving before spending. Left until after spending, saving isn't an action. It is just what's left. Saved first, it is an action. It feels good.

It puts us back on the path.

Save some money now. Take some out of an account where it might be spent and send it to an account where you can invest it.

Step 46: Mindful Spending

It is not possible to be mindful all the time. It might not even be desirable – we may sometimes want to enjoy ourselves with total abandon, being in the moment, whether deliriously happy or in a focused flow state.

What we want is to be mindful at times where being "mindless" might do us harm. There are lots of these, and some are very serious: for our finances, the most serious is probably when we are spending money.

We have already learnt to breathe, to "check in" with how we feel. We have learnt that although money can't actually affect our emotions, we can feel as though it does. The prospect of spending it can make us feel excited, depressed, anxious.

We have also learned that being aware of this is enough. We don't need to tell ourselves anything when we're doing it, good or bad: just be aware.

If you do any shopping today, try to check in with how you feel. Are there any emotions playing with you, making you do things or feel things? Just note what they are – maybe in your secret zen tracker!

Step 47: Investing – Avoiding Scams

Don't be tempted off the path by things that sound too good to be true.

Investment scams are tricky to spot, but one thing they often have in common is that they sound unbelievable. So don't believe them.

If an investment promises high returns without high risks, it is unlikely to be genuine. If the person offering the investment can't explain how the investment makes all these high returns, without the risk those returns don't happen, then don't believe them.

Ask lots of questions.

One thing new investors often forget is that they are now "the boss". Buy the S&P 500 index, and the top 500 CEOs in America now work for you. You can ask them questions – and you can do that before you make any investment.

Anyone offering an investment should be able to answer any question you have, and they should answer it well. They won't tell you not to worry and just sign.

Learn more about this today; moneysavingexpert .com has a great section, that's regularly updated, on how to avoid scams.

Step 48: Owning

Speculating is quick – and it can be over quickly. Anything you do where there is a chance you could lose all your money is basically gambling, and won't lead to ownership. It will lead to nothing.

Investing is the slow process of increasing your ownership. This is another reason why dollar-cost averaging works so well: it rewards steady accumulation of assets.

So target an asset you want to own, a particular amount of an index, for example, or enough for a downpayment on a property, and put a small amount aside towards it.

This is active, so it will make you feel better. And it is building your ownership, of an asset and the process.

Step 49: Now

There is no other time than now.

There is no other time to start. There is no other time to continue.

This does not mean there is no point thinking about the future. On the contrary, now is the time to prepare for a better future, by creating, starting, and building on better habits. Like saving and investing. Like meditation, mindfulness, and breathing.

Like having a calm, mindful, and zen approach to your money.

Go on. Start right now.